SpringerBriefs in Computer Science

More information about this series at http://www.springer.com/series/10028

Lucas Davi • Ahmad-Reza Sadeghi

Building Secure Defenses Against Code-Reuse Attacks

Springer

Lucas Davi
CASED
Technische Universität Darmstadt
Darmstadt, Germany

Ahmad-Reza Sadeghi
CASED
Technische Universität Darmstadt
Darmstadt, Germany

ISSN 2191-5768   ISSN 2191-5776   (electronic)
SpringerBriefs in Computer Science
ISBN 978-3-319-25544-6   ISBN 978-3-319-25546-0   (eBook)
DOI 10.1007/978-3-319-25546-0

Library of Congress Control Number: 2015958780

Springer Cham Heidelberg New York Dordrecht London

Printed on acid-free paper

Springer International Publishing AG Switzerland is part of Springer Science+Business Media (www.springer.com)

Foreword

Exploitation of memory corruption vulnerabilities in widely used software has been a threat for almost three decades, and no end seems to be in sight. In particular, code-reuse techniques such as return-oriented programming are extensively used to exploit memory corruption vulnerabilities in modern software programs, e.g. web browsers, document viewers, or zero-day issues in large-scale cyberattacks such as Stuxnet. Whereas conventional runtime exploits require the injection of malicious code, code-reuse attacks leverage benign code that is already present in the address space of an application to undermine the security model of data execution prevention (DEP). In addition, code-reuse attacks in conjunction with memory disclosure attack techniques circumvent the widely applied memory protection model of address space layout randomization (ASLR). To counter this ingenious attack strategy, a large number of proposals for mitigating these attacks have emerged. In particular, at the time of writing, this field has become a hot topic of research.

In this book, we introduce the problem of code-reuse attacks and explore the limitations of existing defenses. We elaborate on two different defense strategies against code-reuse attacks. First, we explore control-flow integrity enforcement which aims at constraining a program's execution flow to a given control-flow graph (CFG). Second, we introduce the concept of software diversity, focusing particularly on fine-grained code randomization. In contrast to CFI, fine-grained code randomization aims to mitigate code-reuse attacks by randomizing the location where code resides in memory. Both defense approaches have been intensively investigated and integrated into contemporary computing platforms. However, as we will show, both defenses have their limitations that need to be taken into consideration when designing next-generation secure platforms.

Darmstadt, Germany
Lucas Davi
Ahmad-Reza Sadeghi

v

Acknowledgments

This book would have never been possible without the many excellent researchers and coauthors we were privileged to work with over the last few years. In particular, we would like to thank Fabian Monrose, Thorsten Holz, and Yier Jin who have supported us with great feedback.

We'd like to thank our colleagues and coauthors who contributed to many parts of this book: Alexandra Dmitrienko, Marcel Winandy, Christopher Liebchen, Thomas Fischer, Stefan Nürnberger, Mihai Bucicoiu, Stephan Heuser, Ralf Hund, Kevin Z. Snow, Per Larsen, Stephen Crane, Andrei Homescu, Dean Sullivan, Orlando Arias, Mauro Conti, Marco Negro, Stephen Checkoway, Hovav Shacham, Manuel Egele, Blaine Stancill, Nathan Otterness, Felix Schuster, Razvan Deaconescu, and Daniel Lehmann.

We also would like to thank our colleagues at Intel Labs and the Intel Security Institute in Darmstadt (Intel CRI-SC): Anand Rajan, Manoj Sastry, Matthias Schunter, Patrick Koeberl, and Steffen Schulz.

Contents

Chapter 1
Introduction

Computing platforms have become an integral part of our society over the last few decades. The landscape of computing platforms is highly diverse: starting from desktop PCs and laptops for end-users, powerful workstations used to perform highly complex calculations (e.g., weather calculations), web servers that need to simultaneously handle thousands of incoming requests, smartphones and tablets enabling on-the-road data access, up to tiny embedded devices deployed in sensors, cars, electronic passports, and medical devices. The inter-connectivity of these devices, i.e., the Internet of Everything [15], as well as the sensitive operations and everyday tasks we perform on these devices have made computing platforms an appealing target for various attacks. In particular, the fact that devices are connected with each other and to the Internet has facilitated remote attacks, where the attacker does not require any physical hardware access to compromise the victim's platform.

A prominent entry point of remote attacks is a vulnerable software program executing on the target computing platform. In general, computing platforms execute a large number of software programs to operate correctly and meaningful. Modern platforms typically include an operating system kernel (Windows, UNIX/Linux, Mac OS X) as well as user applications that run on top of that operating system, e.g., a web browser, word processor, video player, or a document viewer. Software is written by diverse developers, most of which are not security experts. As a consequence, software indeed operates as expected, but may miss necessary security checks that a sophisticated adversary can exploit to initiate an attack. That is, the adversary provides a malicious input that exploits a program bug to trigger malicious program actions never intended by the developer of the program. This class of software-based attack is generally known as a *runtime exploit* or *control-flow attack*, and needs to be distinguished from conventional *malware* that encapsulates its malicious program actions inside a dedicated executable. This executable simply needs to be executed on the target system and typically requires no exploitation of a program bug. While both runtime exploits and malware are important and prevalent

© The Author(s) 2015
L. Davi, A.-R. Sadeghi, *Building Secure Defenses Against Code-Reuse Attacks*,
SpringerBriefs in Computer Science, DOI 10.1007/978-3-319-25546-0_1

software-based attacks, we mainly focus in this book on runtime exploits, i.e., the art of exploiting benign software programs so that they behave maliciously.

In fact, one of the first large-scale attacks against the Internet contained a runtime exploit: in 1988, the Morris worm affected around 10 % of all computers connected to the Internet disrupting Internet access for several days [5]. The worm exploited a program bug in fingerd—a service (daemon) that allows exchange of status and user information. Specifically, the worm initiated a session with the finger server, and sent a special crafted package that overflowed a local buffer on the stack to (1) inject malicious code on the stack, and (2) overwrite adjacent control-flow information (i.e., a function's return address located on the stack) so that the program's control-flow was redirected to the injected code [32]. Runtime exploits, like the Morris worm, which involve overflowing a buffer are commonly referred to as *buffer overflow attacks*.

The exploitation technique used for the Morris worm is typical for runtime exploits: they first require the exploitation of a program bug to inject malicious code and overwrite control-flow information. In the specific attack against fingerd, the problem is caused by a default C library function called *gets()*. This function reads characters, and stores them into a destination buffer until it reaches a newline character. However, it does not validate whether the input it processes fits to the destination buffer. Hence, a large input will exceed the buffer's bounds, thereby overwriting adjacent information such as a function's return address in memory.

Similar severe attacks have threatened end-users over the last years. In 2001, the so-called Code Red worm infected 250,000 machines within 9 h by exploiting a known buffer overflow vulnerability in Microsoft's Internet Information Server [11]. Another well-known buffer overflow attack is the SQL Slammer worm which infected 75,000 machines in just 10 min causing major Internet slowdowns in 2003 [26].

The continued success of these attacks can be attributed to the fact that large portions of software programs are implemented in type-unsafe languages (C, C++, or Objective-C) that do not enforce bounds checking on data inputs. Moreover, even type-safe languages (e.g., Java) rely on interpreters (e.g., the Java virtual machine) that are in turn implemented in type-unsafe languages. Sadly, as modern compilers and applications become more and more complex, memory errors and vulnerabilities will likely continue to persist, with little end in sight [33, 35].

The most prominent example of a memory error is the stack overflow vulnerability, where the adversary overflows a local buffer on the stack, and overwrites a function's return address [2]. While modern defenses protect against this attack strategy (e.g., by using stack canaries [9]), other avenues for exploitation exists, including those that leverage heap [29], format string [13], or integer overflow [4] vulnerabilities.

Regardless of the attacker's method of choice, exploiting a vulnerability and gaining control over an application's control-flow is only the first step of a runtime exploit. The second step is to launch malicious program actions. Traditionally, this has been realized by injecting malicious code into the application's address space, and later executing the injected code. However, with the wide-spread enforcement of data execution prevention such attacks are more difficult to do today [23]. Unfortunately, the long-held assumption that only code injection posed a risk was shattered with the introduction of *code-reuse attacks*, such as return-into-libc [27, 31] and return-oriented programming [30]. As the name implies, code-reuse attacks do not require any code injection and instead use code already resident in memory.

Code-reuse attack techniques are applicable to a wide range of computing platforms: x86-based platforms [30], embedded systems running on an Atmel AVR processor [12], mobile devices based on ARM [3, 17], PowerPC-based Cisco routers [19], and voting machines deploying a z80 processor [6]. Moreover, the powerful code-reuse attack technique return-oriented programming is Turing-complete, i.e., it allows an attacker to execute arbitrary malicious code.

In fact, the majority of state-of-the-art runtime exploits leverage code-reuse attack techniques, e.g., runtime exploits against Internet Explorer [20, 36], Apple QuickTime [14], Adobe Reader [16], Microsoft Word [7], or the GnuTLS library [37]. Even large-scale cyber attacks such as the popular Stuxnet worm, which damaged Iranian centrifuge rotors, partially deploys code-reuse attack techniques [21].

1.1 Goal and Scope

This book intends to familiarize the reader with the problem of code-reuse attacks against modern software systems and the different defense strategies that have been proposed so far to mitigate these attacks. In general, we focus on defenses that build on the principle of control-flow integrity (CFI) [1] and code randomization [8]. The former provides a generic approach to mitigate runtime exploits by forcing a program's control-flow to always comply to a pre-defined control-flow graph. In contrast, the latter does not perform any explicit control-flow checks. It mitigates code-reuse attacks by randomizing the code layout so that an attacker can hardly predict where useful code resides in memory. As we will discuss throughout this book, both security principles have been intensively explored over the last few years by academia and industry. For instance, Microsoft started a competition, the Microsoft BlueHat Prize, where three CFI-based proposed defenses against return-oriented programming have been awarded with 260k dollars [34]. Its public security tool Microsoft EMET incorporates some of these defenses to mitigate code-reuse attacks [22].

It is important to note that runtime exploits involve two stages: (1) initial control-flow exploitation and (2) malicious program actions. In this book, we focus on the second stage of runtime exploits, i.e., the execution of malicious computations. Modern stack and heap mitigations (such as stack canaries [9] or heap allocation order randomization [28]) do eliminate categories of attacks supporting stage one, but these mitigations are not comprehensive (i.e., exploitable vulnerabilities still exist). Several efforts have been undertaken to achieve memory safety, i.e., preventing any code pointer overwrites for type-unsafe languages [10, 18, 24, 25]. However, these solutions necessarily require access to source code and sometimes incur high performance overhead. Thus, in this book, we assume the adversary is able to exercise one of these pre-existing vulnerable entry points. As a result, a full discussion of the first stage of runtime exploits is out of scope for this book.

1.2 Outline

The remainder of this book is structured as follows: in Chap. 2, we provide comprehensive background information on control-flow attacks covering classic code injection attacks and modern code-reuse attack techniques. Next, in Chap. 3, we introduce the main principles of CFI enforcement. Further, this chapter analyzes the security of recently proposed practical CFI schemes, and elaborates on recent advances in the area of CFI. In Chap. 4, we turn our attention to code randomization schemes. In particular, we demonstrate how just-in-time code-reuse attacks can bypass classic code randomization scheme. Lastly, in Chap. 5 we conclude this book with a comparison on CFI and code randomization.

References

1. Abadi, M., Budiu, M., Erlingsson, U., Ligatti, J.: Control-flow integrity: principles, implementations, and applications. ACM Trans. Inf. Syst. Secur. **13**(1), 4:1–4:40 (2009). http://doi.acm.org/10.1145/1609956.1609960
2. Aleph One: Smashing the stack for fun and profit. Phrack Mag. **49**(14) (2000). http://phrack.org/issues/49/14.html
3. Avraham, I.: Exploitation on ARM - technique and bypassing defense mechanisms. https://www.defcon.org/images/defcon-18/dc-18-presentations/Avraham/DEFCON-18-Avraham-Modern%20ARM-Exploitation-WP.pdf (2010)
4. blexim: Basic integer overflows. Phrack Mag. **60**(10) (2002). http://www.phrack.org/issues.html?issue=60&id=10#article
5. Boettger, L.: The Morris worm: how it affected computer security and lessons learned by it. http://www.giac.org/paper/gsec/405/morris-worm-affected-computer-security-lessons-learned/100954 (2000)
6. Checkoway, S., Feldman, A.J., Kantor, B., Halderman, J.A., Felten, E.W., Shacham, H.: Can DREs provide long-lasting security? The case of return-oriented programming and the AVC advantage. In: Proceedings of the 2009 Conference on Electronic Voting Technology/Workshop on Trustworthy Elections, EVT/WOTE'09 (2009). http://dl.acm.org/citation.cfm?id=1855491.1855497
7. Chen, X., Caselden, D., Scott, M.: The dual use exploit: CVE-2013-3906 used in both targeted attacks and crimeware campaigns. https://www.fireeye.com/blog/threat-research/2013/11/the-dual-use-exploit-cve-2013-3906-used-in-both-targeted-attacks-and-crimeware-campaigns.html (2013)
8. Cohen, F.B.: Operating system protection through program evolution. Comput. Secur. **12**(6), 565–584 (1993). doi:10.1016/0167-4048(93)90054-9

9. Cowan, C., Pu, C., Maier, D., Hintony, H., Walpole, J., Bakke, P., Beattie, S., Grier, A., Wagle, P., Zhang, Q.: StackGuard: automatic adaptive detection and prevention of buffer-overflow attacks. In: Proceedings of the 7th USENIX Security Symposium (1998). http://dl.acm.org/citation.cfm?id=1267549.1267554

10. Cowan, C., Beattie, S., Johansen, J., Wagle, P.: Pointguard: protecting pointers from buffer overflow vulnerabilities. In: Proceedings of the 12th USENIX Security Symposium (2003). http://dl.acm.org/citation.cfm?id=1251353.1251360

11. Danyliw, R., Householder, A.: "Code Red" worm exploiting buffer overflow in IIS indexing service DLL. http://www.cert.org/historical/advisories/ca-2001-19.cfm? (2001)

12. Francillon, A., Castelluccia, C.: Code injection attacks on Harvard-architecture devices. In: Proceedings of the 15th ACM Conference on Computer and Communications Security, CCS'08 (2008). http://doi.acm.org/10.1145/1455770.1455775

13. Gera: Advances in format string exploitation. Phrack Mag. 59(12) (2002). http://www.phrack.com/issues.html?issue=59&id=7

14. Goodin, D.: Apple quicktime backdoor creates code-execution peril. http://www.theregister.co.uk/2010/08/30/apple_quicktime_critical_vuln/ (2010)

15. Greenough, J.: The Internet of everything. http://uk.businessinsider.com/internet-of-everything-2015-bi-2014-12?op=1?r=US (2015)

16. jduck: The latest Adobe exploit and session upgrading. http://bugix-security.blogspot.de/2010/03/adobe-pdf-libtiff-working-exploitcve.html (2010)

17. Kornau, T.: Return oriented programming for the ARM architecture. Master's thesis, Ruhr-University Bochum (2009). http://static.googleusercontent.com/media/www.zynamics.com/en//downloads/kornau-tim--diplomarbeit--rop.pdf

18. Kuznetsov, V., Szekeres, L., Payer, M., Candea, G., Sekar, R., Song, D.: Code-pointer integrity. In: Proceedings of the 11th USENIX Conference on Operating Systems Design and Implementation, OSDI'14 (2014). http://dl.acm.org/citation.cfm?id=2685048.2685061

19. Lindner, F.: Router exploitation. http://www.blackhat.com/presentations/bh-usa-09/LINDNER/BHUSA09-Lindner-RouterExploit-SLIDES.pdf (2009)

20. Marschalek, M.: Dig deeper into the ie vulnerability (cve-2014-1776) exploit. https://www.cyphort.com/dig-deeper-ie-vulnerability-cve-2014-1776-exploit/ (2014)

21. Matrosov, A., Rodionov, E., Harley, D., Malcho, J.: Stuxnet under the microscope. http://www.esetnod32.ru/company/viruslab/analytics/doc/Stuxnet_Under_the_Microscope.pdf (2001)

22. Microsoft: Enhanced Mitigation experience toolkit. https://www.microsoft.com/emet (2015)

23. Microsoft: Data execution prevention (DEP). http://support.microsoft.com/kb/875352/EN-US/ (2006)

24. Nagarakatte, S., Zhao, J., Martin, M.M., Zdancewic, S.: SoftBound: highly compatible and complete spatial memory safety for C. In: Proceedings of the 30th ACM SIGPLAN Conference on Programming Language Design and Implementation, PLDI'09 (2009). http://doi.acm.org/10.1145/1542476.1542504

25. Nagarakatte, S., Zhao, J., Martin, M.M., Zdancewic, S.: Cets: compiler enforced temporal safety for C. In: Proceedings of the 2010 International Symposium on Memory Management, ISMM'10 (2010). http://doi.acm.org/10.1145/1806651.1806657

26. NC State University: What is the Slammer worm/SQL worm/Sapphire worm? https://ethics.csc.ncsu.edu/abuse/wvt/Slammer/study.php (2001)

27. Nergal: The advanced return-into-lib(c) exploits: PaX case study. Phrack Mag. 58(4) (2001). http://www.phrack.org/issues.html?issue=58&id=4#article

28. Novark, G., Berger, E.D.: DieHarder: securing the heap. In: Proceedings of the 17th ACM Conference on Computer and Communications Security, CCS'10 (2010). http://doi.acm.org/10.1145/1866307.1866371

29. Pincus, J., Baker, B.: Beyond stack smashing: recent advances in exploiting buffer overruns. IEEE Secur. Privacy Mag. 2(4), 20–27 (2004). http://dx.doi.org/10.1109/MSP.2004.36

30. Shacham, H.: The geometry of innocent flesh on the bone: return-into-libc without function calls (on the x86). In: Proceedings of the 14th ACM Conference on Computer and Communications Security, CCS'07 (2007). http://doi.acm.org/10.1145/1315245.1315313

31. Solar Designer: lpr LIBC RETURN exploit. http://insecure.org/sploits/linux.libc.return.lpr.
    sploit.html (1997)
32. Spafford, E.H.: The internet worm program: an analysis. SIGCOMM Comput. Commun. Rev.
    19(1), 17–57 (1989). http://doi.acm.org/10.1145/66093.66095
33. Szekeres, L., Payer, M., Wei, T., Song, D.: Sok: Eternal war in memory. In: Proceedings of the
    34th IEEE Symposium on Security and Privacy, SP'13 (2013). http://dx.doi.org/10.1109/SP.
    2013.13
34. Thomlinson, M.: Announcing the BlueHat prize winners. https://blogs.technet.com/b/msrc/
    archive/2012/07/26/announcing-the-bluehat-prize-winners.aspx?Redirected=true (2012)
35. van der Veen, V., dutt-Sharma, N., Cavallaro, L., Bos, H.: Memory errors: the past, the present,
    and the future. In: Proceedings of the 15th International Conference on Research in Attacks,
    Intrusions, and Defenses, RAID'12 (2012). http://dx.doi.org/10.1007/978-3-642-33338-5_5
36. Vreugdenhil, P.: Pwn2Own 2010 Windows 7 Internet Explorer 8 exploit . http://
    vreugdenhilresearch.nl/Pwn2Own-2010-Windows7-InternetExplorer8.pdf (2010)
37. Westin, K.: GnuTLS crypto library vulnerability CVE-2014-3466. http://www.tripwire.com/
    state-of-security/latest-security-news/gnutls-crypto-library-vulnerability-cve-2014-3466/
    (2014)

Chapter 2
Background and Evolution of Code-Reuse Attacks

2.1 General Principle of Control-Flow Attacks

In general, control-flow attacks allow an adversary to subvert the intended execution-flow of a program by exploiting a program error. For instance, a buffer overflow error can be exploited to write data beyond the boundaries of the buffer. As a consequence, an adversary can overwrite critical control-flow information which is located close to the buffer. Since control-flow information guide the program's execution-flow, an adversary can thereby trigger malicious and unintended program actions such as installing a backdoor, injecting a malware, or accessing sensitive data.

Control-flow attacks are performed at application runtime. Hence, they are often referred to as runtime exploits. Note that we use both terms interchangeably in this book. In summary, we define a control-flow attack as follows.

> **Control-Flow Attack (Runtime Exploit):** *A control-flow attack exploits a program error, particularly a memory corruption vulnerability, at application runtime to subvert the intended control-flow of a program. The goal of a control-flow attack is the execution of malicious program actions.*

Loosely speaking, we can distinguish between two major classes of control-flow attacks: (1) code injection and (2) code-reuse attacks. The former class requires the injection of some malicious executable code into the address space of the application. In contrast, code-reuse attacks only leverage benign code already present in the address space of the application. In particular, code-reuse attacks combine small code pieces scattered throughout the address space of the application to generate new malicious program codes on-the-fly.

© The Author(s) 2015
L. Davi, A.-R. Sadeghi, *Building Secure Defenses Against Code-Reuse Attacks*,
SpringerBriefs in Computer Science, DOI 10.1007/978-3-319-25546-0_2

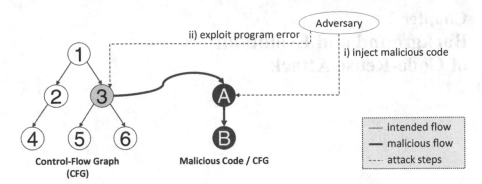

Fig. 2.1 Code injection attacks

A high-level representation of code injection attacks is given in Fig. 2.1. It shows a sample control-flow graph (CFG) with six nodes. The CFG contains all intended execution paths a program might follow at runtime. Typically, the CFG nodes represent the so-called basic blocks (BBLs), where a BBL is a sequence of machine/assembler instructions with a unique entry and exit instruction. The exit instruction can be any branch instruction the processor supports such as direct and indirect jump instructions, direct and indirect call instructions, and function return instructions. The entry instruction of a BBL is an instruction that is target of a branch instruction.

As shown in Fig. 2.1, the CFG nodes are connected via directed edges. These edges represent the possible control-flows, e.g., there is an intended control-flow from node n_3 to n_5 and n_6, where n simply stands for node.

A code injection attack first requires the injection of malicious code. Since programs are allocated into a dedicated memory location at runtime, i.e., the application's virtual address space, the adversary needs to find a free slot to inject her malicious code. Typically, this can be achieved by loading the malicious code into a local buffer that is large enough to hold the entire malicious code. In Fig. 2.1, the malicious code consists of the two nodes n_A and n_B. However, these nodes are not connected to the original CFG. In order to connect the malicious nodes to the intended program nodes, the adversary needs to identify and exploit a program vulnerability. Exploitation of the program vulnerability allows the adversary to tamper with a code pointer, i.e., some control-flow information that guides program execution. A prominent example is a function's return address which is always located on the program stack. Other examples are function pointers or pointers to virtual method tables. In the example exploit shown in Fig. 2.1, n_3 is exploited by the adversary to redirect the execution path to node n_A and n_B. In summary, we define code injection attacks as follows.

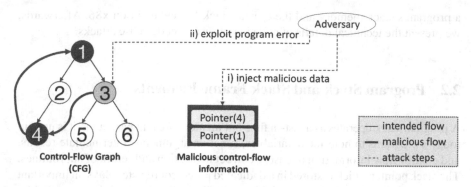

Fig. 2.2 Code-reuse attacks

Code Injection Attack: *A code injection attack is a subclass of control-flow attacks that subverts the intended control-flow of a program to previously injected malicious code.*

Code injection attacks require the injection and execution of malicious code. However, some environments and operating systems deny the execution of code that has just been written into the address space of the program. For instance, a Harvard-based computing architecture strictly separates code and data memory. As a response, a new control-flow attack emerged that only reuses existing code. The high-level principle of these so-called code-reuse attacks is shown in Fig. 2.2.

In contrast to code injection attacks, the adversary only injects malicious data into the address space of the application. Specifically, in the example shown in Fig. 2.2, the adversary injects two code pointers; namely pointers to n_4 and n_1. At the time the adversary exploits the program vulnerability in n_3, the control-flow is redirected to the code pointers the adversary previously injected. Hence, the code-reuse attack in our example leads to the unintended execution path: $n_3 \rightarrow n_4 \rightarrow n_1$. In summary, we define a code-reuse attack as follows.

Code-Reuse Attack: *A code-reuse attack is a subclass of control-flow attacks that subverts the intended control-flow of a program to invoke an unintended execution path inside the original program code.*

Note that the internal workflow and memory layout of a control-flow attack depend on the kind of vulnerability that is exploited. For better understanding, we describe the technical details of control-flow attacks based on a classic buffer overflow vulnerability on the program's stack. Hence, we briefly recall the basics of a program's stack memory and the typical stack frame layout on x86. Afterwards, we present the technical details of code injection and code-reuse attacks.

2.2   Program Stack and Stack Frame Elements

A program stack operates as a last-in first-out memory area. In particular, it is used in today's programs to hold local variables, function arguments, intermediate results, and control-flow information to ensure correct invocation and return of subroutines. The stack pointer which is stored in a dedicated processor register plays an important role because it points to the top of the stack. Typically, the stack is controlled by two operations: (1) a POP instruction that takes one data word off the stack, and (2) a PUSH instruction which performs the reverse operation, i.e., it stores one data word on the top of the stack. Both instructions have direct influence on the stack pointer since they change the top of the stack. That is, for stacks that grow from high memory addresses towards low memory addresses (e.g., x86), the POP instruction automatically increments the stack pointer by one memory word (on x86 by 4 Bytes), while the PUSH instruction decrements it by one word.

In general, the stack is divided into multiple stack frames. Stack frames are associated at function-level, i.e., for each invoked subroutine one stack frame is allocated. The stack frame has a pre-defined structure for each compiler and underlying processor architecture. An example of a typical x86 stack frame and its elements is shown in Fig. 2.3. The depicted stack frame is referenced by two processor registers: the stack pointer (on x86 %esp) and the base pointer register (on x86 %ebp). As we already mentioned, the stack pointer always points to the top of the stack. In contrast to the stack pointer, the base pointer is constant and fixed per stack frame: it always points to the saved base pointer. The meaning of the saved base pointer and the other stack frame elements is as follows:

- **Function Arguments**: This field holds the arguments which are loaded on the stack by the calling function.
- **Return Address**: The return address indicates where the execution-flow needs to be redirected to upon function return. On x86, the instruction for calling a function (CALL) automatically pushes the return address on the stack, where the return address is the address of the instruction that follows the CALL.
- **Saved Base Pointer**: The base pointer of a function is used to reference function arguments and local variables on the stack frame. The function prologue of each subroutine initializes the base pointer. This is achieved in two steps. First, the base pointer of the calling function is pushed onto the stack via PUSH %ebp. The base pointer stored onto the stack is then referred to as the saved base pointer. Next, the new base pointer is initialized by loading the current stack pointer value into the base pointer register, e.g., MOV %ebp,%esp. The function epilogue reverts these operations by first setting the stack pointer to point to the saved

Fig. 2.3 Stack frame
memory layout

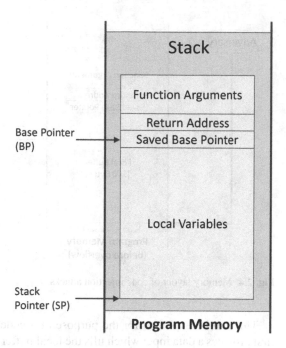

Base Pointer
(BP)

Stack
Pointer (SP)

base pointer field (MOV %esp, %ebp), and subsequently loading the saved base
pointer to the base pointer register via POP %ebp.

- **Local Variables**: The last field of a stack frame holds the local variables such as
  integer values or local buffers.

2.3   Code Injection

In order to perform a code injection attack, the adversary needs to inject malicious
code into the address space of the target application. Typically, this can be achieved
by encapsulating the malicious code into a data input variable that gets processed
by the application, e.g., a string, file, or network packet.

Figure 2.4 depicts a code injection attack, where a local buffer that can hold up
to 100 characters is exploited. The adversary has access to the local buffer, i.e., the
application features a user interface from which it expects the user to enter a data
input. On x86, data is written from low memory addresses towards high memory
addresses, i.e., from the top of the stack towards the saved base pointer in Fig. 2.4.

If the program does not validate the length of the provided data input, it is
possible to provide a larger data input than the buffer can actually hold. As a
consequence, the stack frame fields which are located above the local buffer are
overwritten.

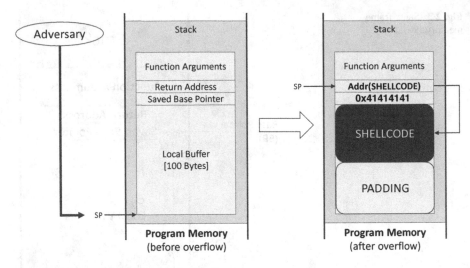

Fig. 2.4 Memory layout of code injection attacks

This can be exploited for the purpose of a code injection attack: the adversary first provides a data input which fills the local buffer with arbitrary pattern bytes and the malicious code. As the main goal of many proof-of-concept exploits is to open a terminal (shell) to the adversary, the malicious code is often referred to as shellcode. Second, the adversary overwrites the saved base pointer with arbitrary bytes (here: 0x41414141) and replaces the original return address with the runtime address of the shellcode. For systems that do not apply code and data segment randomization, this address is fixed, and can be retrieved by reverse-engineering the program binary using a debugger.

When the subroutine—where the overflow occurred—completed its task and executes its function epilogue instructions, the stack pointer will be reset to the location, where the original return address was stored. As the program is not aware of the overflow, it takes the start address of the shellcode as a return address and redirects execution to the beginning of the shellcode. Thus, the shellcode executes and opens a new terminal to the adversary.

2.4 Data Execution Prevention

One main observation we can make from the code injection attack described above is that malicious code can be encapsulated into a data variable and executed from the program's stack. In fact, code injection attacks were easily possible because data and code got intermixed in memory, and not strictly separated as in Harvard-based processor architectures. Hence, data segments like the stack were marked as readable, writable, and executable (RWX). However, since the main purpose of the stack is to only hold local variables and control-flow information, we simply need a mechanism to prohibit any code execution from the stack to prevent a code injection attack. As a consequence, kernel patches have been provided to mark the stack as non-executable [34]; e.g., enabled in Solaris 2.6 [3].

The concept of marking the stack as non-executable has been later included into a more general security model referred to as Writable XOR eXecutable ($W \oplus X$) or data execution prevention (DEP) [29]. The main idea of $W \oplus X$ is to prevent any memory page from being writable and executable at the same time. Hence, memory pages belonging to data segments are marked as readable and writable (RW), whereas memory pages that contain executable code are marked as readable and executable (RX). This effectively prevents code injection attacks since an adversary can no longer execute code that has been written via a data variable to a RW-marked memory page. In summary, we define the principle $W \oplus X$ as follows.

> **Writable xor eXecutable** ($W \oplus X$): *The security model of $W \oplus X$ enforces that memory pages are either marked as writable or executable. This prevents a code injection attack, where the adversary first needs to write malicious code into the address space of an application before executing it.*

Today, every mainstream processor architecture features the so-called no-execute bit to facilitate the deployment of $W \oplus X$ in modern operating systems. For instance, Windows-based operating systems enforce DEP since Windows XP SP2 [29].

2.5 Code-Reuse Attacks

After non-executable stacks and $W \oplus X$ have been proposed as countermeasures against control-flow attacks, attackers have instantly demonstrated new techniques to launch control-flow attacks. Instead of injecting malicious code into the address space of the application, an adversary can exploit the benign code which is already present in the address space and marked as executable. Such code-reuse attacks have started as so-called return-into-libc attacks and have been later generalized to return-oriented programming attacks. We describe the technical concepts of both attack techniques in the following.

2.5.1 Return-Into-Libc

The first published exploit that reuses existing code for a return-into-libc attack has been presented by Solar Designer in 1997 [33]. The exploit overwrites the original return address to point to a critical library function. Specifically, it targets the *system()* function of the standard UNIX C library `libc`, which is linked to nearly every process running on a UNIX-based system. The *system()* function takes as an input a shell command to be executed. For instance, on UNIX-based systems the function call *system("/bin/sh")* opens the terminal program. That said, by invoking the *system()* function, the adversary can conveniently reconstruct the operations of previously injected shellcode without injecting any code. In summary, we define a return-into-libc attack as follows.

Return-Into-Libc: *Code-reuse attacks that are based on the principle of return-into-libc subvert the intended control-flow of a program and redirect it to security-critical functions that reside in shared libraries or the executable itself.*

Figure 2.5 shows the typical memory layout of a return-into-libc attack. A necessary step of our specific return-into-libc attack is the injection of the string /bin/sh since *system()* is expecting a pointer to the program path in order to open a new terminal. To tackle this issue, one could search for the string inside the

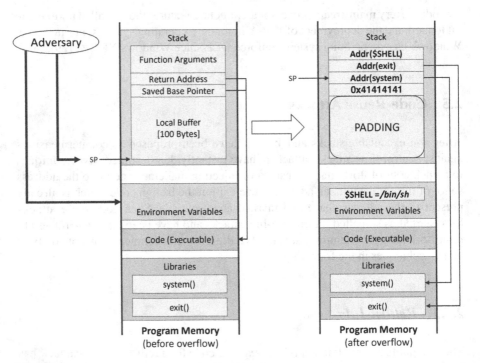

Fig. 2.5 Basic principle of return-into-libc attacks

entire address space of the target application. However, this approach is unreliable as the string might not always be present in the address space of the application. A more robust exploitation approach is to inject the string into a data memory page and record its address. At first glance, this might seem a trivial step. However, the challenge stems from the fact that the string needs to be NULL-terminated. Hence, if we attempt to inject the string into the local buffer, we would need to process a NULL Byte which is impossible for many vulnerabilities. For instance, classic buffer overflow vulnerabilities introduced via the *strcpy()* function terminate the write operation if a NULL Byte is processed. The classic return-into-libc attacks overcome this issue by injecting the string as an environment variable. In Fig. 2.5, the adversary defines the $SHELL environment variable which contains the string /bin/sh.

After the environment variable has been defined, the adversary interfaces to the application by providing a data input that exceeds the local buffer's limits. Specifically, the adversary fills the local buffer with arbitrary pattern bytes. In addition, the saved base pointer is overwritten with 4 Bytes of arbitrary data. Finally, the return address is replaced with the runtime address of the *system()* function. Moreover, two other addresses are written on the stack: the runtime address of the libc *exit()* function, and the runtime address of the $SHELL variable. The latter resembles the function argument on the stack frame of the invoked *system()* function. Considering the standard x86-based stack frame layout (see Fig. 2.3), the former will be used as the return address of *system()*. In particular, the *exit()* function will terminate the process upon return of *system()*, i.e., at the time the adversary closes the terminal.

This basic return-into-libc attack requires the knowledge of three runtime addresses. In case no code and data randomization is applied, these addresses can be retrieved by reverse-engineering the application using a debugger. Otherwise, an adversary would need to disclose these addresses using memory disclosure techniques which we discuss in detail in Chap. 4.

The basic return-into-libc attacks only allow invocation of two library library functions, while the second function (in Fig. 2.5 the *exit()* function) needs to be called without any argument. As this poses restrictions on the operations an adversary can perform, several advanced return-into-libc attack techniques have been proposed. For instance, Nergal demonstrated two techniques, called esp-lifting and frame faking, allowing an adversary to perform chained function calls in a return-into-libc attack [30].

2.5.2 Return-Oriented Programming

The above described return-into-libc attack technique has some limitations compared to classic code injection attacks. First, an adversary is dependent on critical libc functions such as *system()*, *exec()*, or *open()*. Hence, if we either instrument or eliminate these functions, an adversary would no longer be able to perform a reasonable attack. In fact, one of the first proposed defenses against return-into-libc is based on the idea of mapping shared libraries to memory addresses that always contain a NULL byte [33]. Second, return-into-libc only allows calling one function after each other. Hence, an adversary is not able to perform arbitrary malicious computation. In particular, it is not possible to perform unconditional branching.

There is also a challenge when applying return-into-libc attacks to 64 Bit based systems (x86-64). On x86-64, function arguments are passed to a subroutine via processor registers rather than on the stack. To tackle this challenge, Krahmer [23] suggested an advanced return-into-libc attack technique called borrowed code chunks exploitation. The main idea is to borrow a function epilogue consisting of several POP register instructions. These instructions load the necessary function arguments into processor registers and subsequently redirect the execution-flow to the target subroutine.

Shacham generalizes the idea of borrowed code chunks exploitation by introducing return-oriented programming. This attack technique tackles the previously mentioned limitations of return-into-libc attacks. The basic idea is to execute a chain of short code sequences rather than entire functions. Multiple code sequences are combined to a so-called gadget that performs a specific atomic task, e.g., a load, add, or branch operation. Given a sufficiently large code base, an adversary will most likely identify a gadget set that forms a new Turing-complete language. That said, the derived gadget set can be exploited to induce arbitrary malicious program behavior. The applicability of return-oriented programming has been shown on many platforms including x86 [32], SPARC [4], Atmel AVR [14], PowerPC [25], ARM [22], and z80 [5].

The basic idea and workflow of a return-oriented programming attack is shown in Fig. 2.6. Note that we discuss a return-oriented programming attack that exploits a heap-based vulnerability to explain all basic attack steps that are taken in modern real-world code-reuse exploits. First, the adversary writes the return-oriented payload into the application's memory space, where the payload mainly consists of a number of pointers (the return addresses) and any other data that is needed for running the attack (Step ①). In particular, the payload is placed into a memory area that can be controlled by the adversary, i.e., the area is writable and the adversary knows its start address. The next step is to exploit a vulnerability of the target program to hijack the intended execution-flow (Step ②). In the example shown in Fig. 2.6, the adversary exploits a heap vulnerability by overwriting the address of a function pointer with an address that points to a so-called *stack pivot* sequence [39]. Once the overwritten function pointer is used by the application, the execution-flow is redirected to a stack pivot sequence (Step ③).

Loosely speaking, stack pivot sequences change the value of the stack pointer (%esp) to a value stored in another register. Hence, by controlling that register,[1] the

---

[1]To control the register, the adversary can either use a buffer overflow exploit that overwrites memory areas that are used to load the target register, or invoke a sequence that initializes the target register and then directly calls the stack pivot.

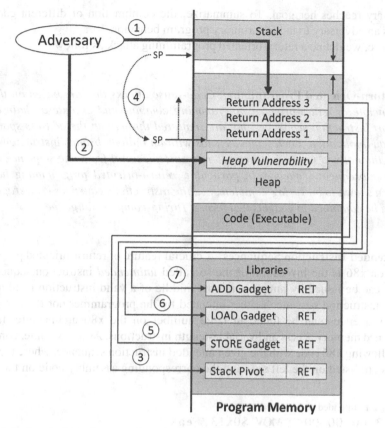

Fig. 2.6 Basic principle of return-oriented programming attacks. For simplicity, we highlight a return-oriented programming attack on the heap using a sequence of single-instruction gadgets

adversary can arbitrarily change the stack pointer. Typically, the stack pivot directs the stack pointer to the beginning of the payload (Step ④). A concrete example of a stack pivot sequence is the x86 assembler code sequence MOV %esp,%eax; ret. The sequence changes the value of the stack pointer to the value stored in register %eax and subsequently invokes a return (RET) instruction. Notice that the stack pivot sequence ends in a RET instruction: the x86 RET instruction simply loads the address pointed to by %esp into the instruction pointer and increments %esp by one word. Hence, the execution continues at the first gadget (STORE) pointed to by Return Address 1 (Step ⑤). In addition, the stack pointer is increased and now points to Return Address 2.

It is exactly the terminating RET instruction that enables the chained execution of gadgets by loading the address the stack pointer points to (Return Address 2) in the instruction pointer and updating the stack pointer so that it points to the next address in the payload (Return Address 3). Steps ⑤ to ⑦ are repeated until the adversary reaches her goal. To summarize, the combination of different gadgets allows an adversary to induce arbitrary program behavior.

Hence, we define a return-oriented programming attack as follows.

> **Return-Oriented Programming**: *Code-reuse attacks that are based on the principle of return-oriented programming combine and execute a chain of short instruction sequences that are scattered throughout the address space of an application. Each sequence ends with an indirect branch instruction—traditionally, a return instruction—to transfer control from one sequence to the subsequent sequence. In particular, return-oriented programming has been shown to be Turing-complete, i.e., the instruction sequences it leverages can be combined to gadgets that form a Turing-complete language.*

Unintended Instruction Sequences A crucial feature of return-oriented programming on x86 is the invocation of the so-called *unintended* instruction sequences. These can be issued by jumping into the middle of a valid instruction resulting in a new instruction sequence neither intended by the programmer nor the compiler. Such sequences can be found in large number on the x86 architecture due to unaligned memory access and variable-length instructions. As an example, consider the following x86 code with the given intended instruction sequence, where the byte values are listed on the left side and the corresponding assembly code on the right side:

Listing 2.1 Intended code sequence
```
b8  13  00  00  00      MOV  $0x13,%eax
e9  c3  f8  ff  ff       JMP  3aae9
```

If the interpretation of the byte stream starts two bytes later the following unintended instruction sequence would be executed:

Listing 2.2 Unintended code sequence
```
00  00      ADD  %al , (%eax )
00  e9      ADD  %ch,% cl
c3          RET
```

In the intended instruction sequence the c3 byte is part of the second instruction. However, if the interpretation starts two bytes later, the c3 byte will be interpreted as a return instruction.

2.6 Hybrid Exploits

Typically, modern systems enforce $W \oplus X$ by default. This forces an adversary to deploy code-reuse attacks. However, a deeper investigation of real-world code-reuse attacks quickly reveals that most exploits today use a combination of code-reuse and

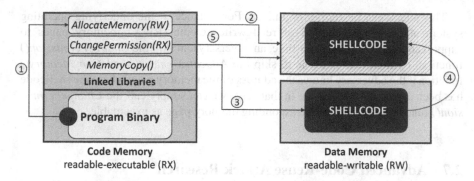

Fig. 2.7 Hybrid exploitation: combination of code-reuse with code injection

code injection. The main idea behind these hybrid exploits is to only use code-reuse attack techniques to undermine $W \oplus X$ protection and launch a code injection attack subsequently. This is possible due to the fact that $W \oplus X$ in its basic instantiation only enforces that a memory page is not writable and executable at the same time. However, a memory page can be first writable (not-executable) and at a later time executable (not-writable).

Figure 2.7 demonstrates this combined attack technique by example. The shown memory layout is divided into a code and data memory area, where the former one is readable and executable, and the latter one is marked as readable and writable. In particular, the code memory holds the program binary and linked shared libraries. In modern operating systems, several important libraries and their functionality are linked by default into the address space of the application. Consider as an example the UNIX C library libc. Although the target application may only require the *printf()* function to print strings on the standard output (stdout), other libc functions such as *system()* or *memcpy()* will be always mapped into the address space of the application as well.

In our example, we assume that the return-oriented payload and the malicious code have been already injected into the data memory area. In Step ①, the payload exploits a program vulnerability and redirects execution to the shared library segment. Specifically, the adversary invokes a default function to allocate a new memory page (e.g., the *alloc()* function) marked as readable and writable (Step ②). Typically, the return value will be the runtime address of the newly allocated page. Upon return of the memory allocator, the return-oriented payload invokes a memory copy function (e.g., the *memcpy()* function) to copy the injected shellcode to the newly allocated memory page (Step ③ and ④). Finally, the payload invokes a system function (e.g., the *mprotect()* function) to change the memory page permissions of the newly allocated page to readable and executable (Step ⑤). Hence, the adversary can now execute the injected shellcode to perform the actual malicious program actions.

This attack can be further optimized. For instance, if the underlying operating system allows the allocation of read–write-execute (RWX) memory pages to support code generation just-in-time, an adversary can skip the *ChangePermission()* function. Further, it is possible to skip the *AllocateMemory()* and *CopyMemory()* function if the adversary knows the address of the memory page where the shellcode has been originally injected to. In that case, we can simply call the *ChangePermission()* function to mark the corresponding memory page as executable.

2.7 Advanced Code-Reuse Attack Research

Subsequent work demonstrated that Harvard-based architectures—where code and data are strictly separated from each other—cannot prevent return-oriented programming attacks. To this end, Francillon and Castelluccia [14] leverage return-oriented programming to inject arbitrary malware on an Atmel AVR-powered sensor. Further, Buchanan et al. [4] apply return-oriented programming to the RISC-based architecture SPARC, where no unintended code sequences exist by design. In particular, they introduce a compiler that automatically constructs return-oriented exploits. In a similar vein, return-oriented programming has been shown on other architectures including PowerPC-based Cisco routers [25] and ARM-based mobile devices [20, 22]. As real-world example, Checkoway et al. [5] even demonstrate a return-oriented programming exploit on z80-powered voting machines (Harvard architecture) to shift votes.

Hund et al. [19] go one step further: they present the first compiler that automatically identifies return-oriented gadgets in a given binary and compiles (based on the gadget set) return-oriented programs. In particular, they construct a kernel rootkit that entirely leverages return-oriented programming to undermine kernel integrity protection mechanisms. Interestingly, the evaluation of the return-oriented compiler reveals that quicksort executes more than 100 times slower when entirely implemented as return-oriented program. Unfortunately, none of the countermeasures proposed to date has further investigated the tremendous performance overhead of return-oriented programming which could potentially be exploited to detect return-oriented programming execution.

On the one hand, return-oriented programming raised a lot of academic and industrial research. On the other hand, no real-world exploits using return-oriented programming have been discovered until 2010. We believe that this is due to the fact that many PC platforms still did not strictly enforce DEP thereby allowing attackers to launch conventional code injection attacks. However, in 2010, the first return-oriented exploit targeting Adobe PDF has been discovered [21]. From there on, a number of return-oriented exploits have appeared [9, 16, 28, 38].

More distantly related to return-oriented programming is the concept of JIT-spraying attacks [1]. These attacks allow an adversary to return to code she injected via a script. This is achieved by forcing a JIT-compiler to allocate new executable memory pages with attacker-defined code that encapsulates dangerous unintended instruction sequences. Since scripting languages do not permit an adversary to directly program x86 shellcode, the attacker must carefully construct the script so that it contains useful gadgets in the form of unintended instruction sequences. For instance, Blazakis [1] suggests using XOR operations where the immediate operand to the XOR instruction embeds the malicious instructions. In a recent work, Wilson et al. [24] demonstrate that JIT-spraying attacks are also applicable to architectures that are based on an ARM processor.

2.7.1 Jump-Oriented Programming

All conventional return-oriented programming attacks discussed so far are based on return instructions and thus can be defeated by return address checkers. These tools or compiler extensions ensure the integrity of return addresses, which are corrupted through the conventional return-oriented programming attack [10–12, 15, 17]. However, Checkoway et al. [6] propose a new code-reuse attack that does not require any return instruction. Instead, the attack exploits indirect jump and call instructions on x86 and ARM-based platforms.

Similarly, Bletsch et al. [2] introduce jump-oriented programming (on x86), a code-reuse attack that also requires no return instructions. Bletsch et al. [2] leverage a generic dispatcher gadget to transfer control to the subsequent code sequence. Chen et al. [7] leverage jump-oriented programming to construct a rootkit that does not execute any return instruction.

2.7.2 Gadget Compilers

Gadget compilers ease the adversary's job of identifying gadgets in a given binary, and constructing a return-oriented exploit thereof. We already mentioned two of these gadget compilers: Buchanan et al. [4] introduce a return-oriented exploit compiler for SPARC, and Hund et al. [19] a gadget compiler that automatically identifies gadgets and compiles a return-oriented exploit for x86. However, these two gadget compilers focus on code sequences ending in a return instruction. A gadget compiler that entirely focuses on constructing jump-oriented exploits is presented by Chen et al. [8]. The compiler targets x86-compiled code and leverages the so-called combinational gadget terminating in a CALL-JMP sequence to invoke a system call in a jump-oriented attack. Whereas the previously discussed gadget compilers focused on a particular processor platform, Dullien et al. [13] introduce a gadget discovery tool that operates platform-independent by decompiling assembler instructions to an intermediate language called REIL.

Lastly, Schwartz et al. [31] present the Q compiler. This compiler automates the entire process of identifying gadgets, assembling a return-oriented exploit, and hardening existing exploits that fail due to code randomization or DEP. Interestingly, the Q compiler is based on semantic definitions, e.g., it considers $reg_1 \leftarrow reg_2 * 1$ as a data movement gadget rather than a multiplication gadget allowing Q to compensate missing gadget types. This technique allows Q to generate return-oriented exploits on a small code base (e.g., 20 KB code) that does not per-se contain all gadget types. Related to the small code base leveraged by Schwartz et al. [31], Homescu et al. [18] demonstrate that a Turing-complete gadget set can be derived from so-called microgadgets, i.e., code sequences that only consist of 2–3 Bytes. The probability of finding these very short sequences among different binaries is higher than compared to complex gadgets.

2.7.3   Code-Reuse in Malware

Code-reuse attack techniques have been also leveraged to hide malicious program behavior from static analysis tools or non-ASCII filters. Lu et al. [26] leverage a return-oriented decoder that only consists of code pointers that represent valid ASCII printable characters. The decoder takes as an input the encoded code-reuse exploit and outputs the actual code-reuse exploit at application runtime. Similarly, Wang et al. [37] successfully deployed code-reuse attack techniques to undermine the application vetting process conducted by Apple. To this end, they developed an application that contains an intended buffer overflow vulnerability which gets exploited under certain conditions (e.g., after the app is installed on the user's device). Once the control-flow is hijacked, the exploit payload leverages return-oriented programming to invoke private iOS APIs. Lastly, Vogl et al. [36] introduce persistent data-only malware, i.e., malware that leverages code-reuse attack techniques to realize a persistent rootkit. With respect to malware detection, Stancill et al. [35] present an analysis system that detects return-oriented programming payloads in malicious files. Their system efficiently analyzes incoming documents (PDF, Office, or HTML files), and detects whether they contain a return-oriented programming payload.

In a different domain, code-reuse techniques have been deployed to hide secret program actions: Lu et al. [27] introduce program steganography that is based on executing unintended code sequences to hide program actions from static analysis tools. However, leveraging code-reuse attack techniques for a legitimate and benign purpose will eventually lead to false alarms in tools that aim at detecting and preventing code-reuse attacks.

This concludes our discussion on research on code-reuse attacks. However, note that we will discuss more advanced code-reuse attacks in the subsequent chapters. In particular, we will elaborate on those attacks that bypass defenses based on control-flow integrity enforcement or fine-grained code randomization.

References

1. Blazakis, D.: Interpreter exploitation. In: Proceedings of the 4th USENIX Conference on Offensive Technologies, WOOT'10 (2010). http://dl.acm.org/citation.cfm?id=1925004. 1925011
2. Bletsch, T., Jiang, X., Freeh, V.W., Liang, Z.: Jump-oriented programming: a new class of code-reuse attack. In: Proceedings of the 6th ACM Symposium on Information, Computer and Communications Security, ASIACCS'11 (2011). http://doi.acm.org/10.1145/1966913. 1966919
3. Brunette, G.: Solaris non-executable stack overview. https://blogs.oracle.com/gbrunett/entry/solaris_non_executable_stack_overview (2007)
4. Buchanan, E., Roemer, R., Shacham, H., Savage, S.: When good instructions go bad: generalizing return-oriented programming to RISC. In: Proceedings of the 15th ACM Conference on Computer and Communications Security, CCS'08 (2008). http://doi.acm.org/10.1145/1455770.1455776
5. Checkoway, S., Feldman, A.J., Kantor, B., Halderman, J.A., Felten, E.W., Shacham, H.: Can DREs provide long-lasting security? The case of return-oriented programming and the AVC advantage. In: Proceedings of the 2009 Conference on Electronic Voting Technology/-Workshop on Trustworthy Elections, EVT/WOTE'09 (2009). http://dl.acm.org/citation.cfm?id=1855491.1855497
6. Checkoway, S., Davi, L., Dmitrienko, A., Sadeghi, A.R., Shacham, H., Winandy, M.: Return-oriented programming without returns. In: Proceedings of the 17th ACM Conference on Computer and Communications Security, CCS'10 (2010). http://doi.acm.org/10.1145/1866307.1866370
7. Chen, P., Xing, X., Mao, B., Xie, L.: Return-oriented rootkit without returns (on the x86). In: Information and Communications Security. Lecture Notes in Computer Science, vol. 6476 (2010). http://link.springer.com/chapter/10.1007%2F978-3-642-17650-0_24
8. Chen, P., Xing, X., Mao, B., Xie, L., Shen, X., Yin, X.: Automatic construction of jump-oriented programming shellcode (on the x86). In: Proceedings of the 6th ACM Symposium on Information, Computer and Communications Security, ASIACCS'11 (2011). http://doi.acm.org/10.1145/1966913.1966918
9. Chen, X., Caselden, D., Scott, M.: The dual use exploit: CVE-2013-3906 used in both targeted attacks and crimeware campaigns. https://www.fireeye.com/blog/threat-research/2013/11/the-dual-use-exploit-cve-2013-3906-used-in-both-targeted-attacks-and-crimeware-campaigns. html (2013)
10. Chiueh, T., Hsu, F.H.: RAD: a compile-time solution to buffer overflow attacks. In: Proceedings of the 21st International Conference on Distributed Computing Systems, ICDCS'01 (2001). http://dl.acm.org/citation.cfm?id=876878.879316
11. Chiueh, T., Prasad, M.: A binary rewriting defense against stack based overflow attacks. In: Proceedings of the 2003 USENIX Annual Technical Conference, ATC'03 (2003). https://www. usenix.org/legacy/event/usenix03/tech/full_papers/prasad/prasad_html/camera.html
12. Davi, L., Sadeghi, A.R., Winandy, M.: ROPdefender: a detection tool to defend against return-oriented programming attacks. In: Proceedings of the 6th ACM Symposium on Information, Computer and Communications Security, ASIACCS'11 (2011). http://doi.acm.org/10.1145/1966913.1966920
13. Dullien, T., Kornau, T., Weinmann, R.P.: A framework for automated architecture-independent gadget search. In: Proceedings of the 4th USENIX Conference on Offensive Technologies, WOOT'10 (2010). http://dl.acm.org/citation.cfm?id=1925004.1925012
14. Francillon, A., Castelluccia, C.: Code injection attacks on Harvard-architecture devices. In: Proceedings of the 15th ACM Conference on Computer and Communications Security, CCS'08 (2008). http://doi.acm.org/10.1145/1455770.1455775
15. Frantzen, M., Shuey, M.: StackGhost: hardware facilitated stack protection. In: Proceedings of the 10th USENIX Security Symposium (2001). http://dl.acm.org/citation.cfm?id=1251327. 1251332

16. Goodin, D.: Apple quicktime backdoor creates code-execution peril. http://www.theregister.co.uk/2010/08/30/apple_quicktime_critical_vuln/ (2010)
17. Gupta, S., Pratap, P., Saran, H., Arun-Kumar, S.: Dynamic code instrumentation to detect and recover from return address corruption. In: Proceedings of the 2006 International Workshop on Dynamic Systems Analysis, WODA'06, pp. 65–72 (2006). http://doi.acm.org/10.1145/1138912.1138926
18. Homescu, A., Stewart, M., Larsen, P., Brunthaler, S., Franz, M.: Microgadgets: size does matter in Turing-complete return-oriented programming. In: Proceedings of the 6th USENIX Conference on Offensive Technologies, WOOT'12 (2012). http://dl.acm.org/citation.cfm?id=2372399.2372409
19. Hund, R., Holz, T., Freiling, F.C.: Return-oriented rootkits: bypassing kernel code integrity protection mechanisms. In: Proceedings of the 18th Conference on USENIX Security Symposium (2009). http://dl.acm.org/citation.cfm?id=1855768.1855792
20. Iozzo, V., Miller, C.: Fun and games with Mac OS X and iPhone payloads. In: Black Hat Europe (2009). http://www.blackhat.com/presentations/bh-europe-09/Miller_Iozzo/BlackHat-Europe-2009-Miller-Iozzo-OSX-IPhone-Payloads-whitepaper.pdf
21. jduck: The latest Adobe exploit and session upgrading. http://bugix-security.blogspot.de/2010/03/adobe-pdf-libtiff-working-exploitcve.html (2010)
22. Kornau, T.: Return oriented programming for the ARM architecture. Master's thesis, Ruhr-University Bochum (2009). http://static.googleusercontent.com/media/www.zynamics.com/en//downloads/kornau-tim--diplomarbeit--rop.pdf
23. Krahmer, S.: x86-64 buffer overflow exploits and the borrowed code chunks exploitation technique. http://users.suse.com/~krahmer/no-nx.pdf (2005)
24. Lian, W., Shacham, H., Savage, S.: Too lejit to quit: extending JIT spraying to ARM. In: 22nd Annual Network and Distributed System Security Symposium, NDSS'15 (2015). http://www.internetsociety.org/doc/too-lejit-quit-extending-jit-spraying-arm
25. Lindner, F.: Router exploitation. http://www.blackhat.com/presentations/bh-usa-09/LINDNER/BHUSA09-Lindner-RouterExploit-SLIDES.pdf (2009)
26. Lu, K., Zou, D., Wen, W., Gao, D.: Packed, printable, and polymorphic return-oriented programming. In: Proceedings of the 14th International Conference on Recent Advances in Intrusion Detection, RAID'11 (2011). http://dx.doi.org/10.1007/978-3-642-23644-0_6
27. Lu, K., Xiong, S., Gao, D.: Ropsteg: program steganography with return oriented programming. In: Proceedings of the 4th ACM Conference on Data and Application Security and Privacy, CODASPY'14 (2014). http://doi.acm.org/10.1145/2557547.2557572
28. Marschalek, M.: Dig deeper into the ie vulnerability (cve-2014-1776) exploit. https://www.cyphort.com/dig-deeper-ie-vulnerability-cve-2014-1776-exploit/ (2014)
29. Microsoft: Data execution prevention (DEP). http://support.microsoft.com/kb/875352/EN-US/ (2006)
30. Nergal: The advanced return-into-lib(c) exploits: PaX case study. Phrack Mag. 58(4) (2001). http://www.phrack.org/issues.html?issue=58&id=4#article
31. Schwartz, E.J., Avgerinos, T., Brumley, D.: Q: Exploit hardening made easy. In: Proceedings of the 20th USENIX Security Symposium (2011). http://dl.acm.org/citation.cfm?id=2028067.2028092
32. Shacham, H.: The geometry of innocent flesh on the bone: return-into-libc without function calls (on the x86). In: Proceedings of the 14th ACM Conference on Computer and Communications Security, CCS'07 (2007). http://doi.acm.org/10.1145/1315245.1315313
33. Solar Designer: lpr LIBC RETURN exploit. http://insecure.org/sploits/linux.libc.return.lpr.sploit.html (1997)
34. Solar Designer: Non-executable stack patch. http://lkml.iu.edu/hypermail/linux/kernel/9706.0/0341.html (1997)
35. Stancill, B., Snow, K., Otterness, N., Monrose, F., Davi, L., Sadeghi, A.R.: Check my profile: leveraging static analysis for fast and accurate detection of rop gadgets. In: Research in Attacks, Intrusions, and Defenses. Lecture Notes in Computer Science, vol. 8145 (2013). http://dx.doi.org/10.1007/978-3-642-41284-4_4

36. Vogl, S., Pfoh, J., Kittel, T., Eckert, C.: Persistent data-only malware: function hooks without code. In: Proceedings of the 21st Annual Network and Distributed System Security Symposium, NDSS'14 (2014). http://www.internetsociety.org/doc/persistent-data-only-malware-function-hooks-without-code
37. Wang, T., Lu, K., Lu, L., Chung, S., Lee, W.: Jekyll on iOS: when benign apps become evil. In: Proceedings of the 22nd USENIX Security Symposium (2013). http://dl.acm.org/citation.cfm?id=2534766.2534814
38. Westin, K.: GnuTLS crypto library vulnerability CVE-2014-3466. http://www.tripwire.com/state-of-security/latest-security-news/gnutls-crypto-library-vulnerability-cve-2014-3466/ (2014)
39. Zovi, D.D.: Practical return-oriented programming. SOURCE Boston. http://trailofbits.files.wordpress.com/2010/04/practical-rop.pdf (2010)

Chapter 3
Building Control-Flow Integrity Defenses

3.1 Basics of Control-Flow Integrity Enforcement

Basics of control-flow integrity (CFI) enforces that a program's control-flow always follows a legitimate path in the application's control-flow graph (CFG) [2, 4]. Figure 3.1 shows a high-level representation of CFI: first, and prior to program execution, the application's CFG needs to be identified. Next, a CFI check is emitted at the exit instruction of each CFG node. These CFI checks are executed at runtime to prevent any attempt of the adversary to hijack the program's control-flow. For instance, the CFI check at node n_3 validates that the exit instruction only targets either n_5 or n_6. If the adversary aims to redirect execution to n_4, CFI will immediately terminate the program execution. In summary, we define CFI as follows.

> **Control-Flow Integrity (CFI)**: *CFI offers a generic defense against code-reuse attacks by validating the integrity of a program's control-flow based on a pre-defined CFG at runtime.*

In particular, Abadi et al. [2, 4] suggest a label-based CFI approach, where each CFG node is marked with a unique label ID that is placed at the beginning of a BBL. In order to preserve the program's original semantics, the label is either encoded as an offset into a x86 cache prefetch instruction or as simple data word. Inserting labels into a program binary will require moving instructions from their original position. As a consequence, CFI requires adjusting all memory offsets embedded into jump/call and data load/store instructions that are affected by the insertion of the additional prefetch instructions. Originally, CFI on x86 builds upon the binary

© The Author(s) 2015
L. Davi, A.-R. Sadeghi, *Building Secure Defenses Against Code-Reuse Attacks*,
SpringerBriefs in Computer Science, DOI 10.1007/978-3-319-25546-0_3

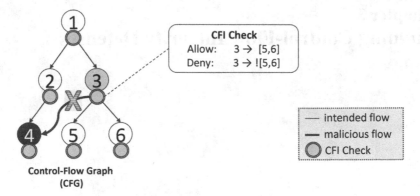

Fig. 3.1 Control-flow integrity (CFI)

instrumentation framework Vulcan which provides algorithms to derive the CFG and a binary rewriting engine to emit labels and CFI checks without breaking the original program-flow.

CFI builds upon several assumptions to effectively defend against code-reuse attacks. Foremost, it assumes that code is not writable, and that an adversary cannot execute injected code from data memory. Both is ensured by enforcing the $W \oplus X$ security model which is enabled by default on modern operating systems (cf. Sect. 2.4). However, this also means that original CFI is not applicable to self-modifying code, or code that is generated just-in-time.

As code is assumed to be immutable, Abadi et al. [2, 4] take an optimization step to increase the efficiency of CFI: they only emit and perform CFI checks for nodes that terminate with an indirect branch instruction. In contrast, direct branch instructions use a statically encoded offset that cannot be altered by an adversary. In the following, we discuss in more detail the general usage scenario for different kinds of indirect branches and how CFI checks are implemented for them.

3.1.1 CFI for Indirect Jumps

Typically, indirect jumps are emitted by the compiler for (1) switch-case statements and (2) dispatch of subroutine calls to shared libraries. We will describe both usage scenarios before we show how CFI protects this type of indirect branch.

A switch-case statement allows a programmer to execute code based on the content of a variable which is checked against a list of pre-defined values. An example of a switch-case statement that consists of three case branches is shown on the left-hand site of Fig. 3.2. These branches are reached using an indirect jump instruction based on the content of the variable `value` that can hold the numbers 1, 2, or 3.

On assembler level, the content of `value` is loaded to register `eax`. The same register is later used in an indirect jump instruction to redirect the control-flow to

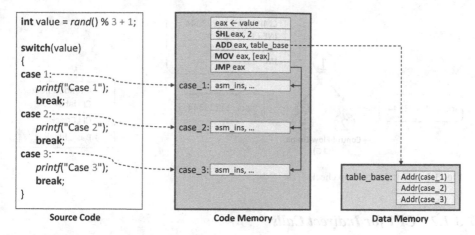

Fig. 3.2 Indirect jumps in switch-case statements

one of the case branches. The main idea is to load the correct target address from a dedicated jump table based on the content of value. For this, the program performs as follows: first, eax is left-shifted via SHL by 2 Bits. This is necessary to correctly load the correct target address from the 4-Byte aligned jump table that contains the three possible case branch target addresses. As a result, the base address of the table is added to eax after the left shift. Lastly, eax is de-referenced to load the target branch address into eax. The subsequent indirect jump takes the address stored in eax to invoke the correct case statement. Register eax can potentially be controlled by an adversary, e.g., a buffer overflow is exploited to alter value. Hence, it is crucial to perform a CFI check before the indirect jump is executed.

Indirect jumps can also take their target address directly from memory. A prominent example is the dispatch of subroutine calls to shared libraries: consider an application that invokes *printf()* from libc. The runtime address of *printf()* will be loaded at a designated memory location in the global offset table (GOT). The function call to *printf()* in the main application goes through an indirection using the so-called procedure linkage table (PLT). The PLT contains stub code that eventually executes an indirect jump that uses as its target address the runtime address located in the GOT. However, an adversary may exploit a memory-related vulnerability to corrupt the value in the GOT thereby hijacking the intended control-flow.

Figure 3.3 demonstrates how CFI protects indirect jumps from being exploited. In our example, n_1 invokes an indirect jump based on the value stored in eax. Note that n_1 is only allowed to target n_2 and n_3. Hence, CFI needs to emit the unique label 11223344 at the beginning of n_2 and n_3. The exit instruction of n_1 is instrumented in such a way that dedicated CFI code validates whether eax targets the label 11223344. Only if this is the case, the program is allowed to take the indirect jump. As the label occupies 4-Byte in memory at n_2 and n_3, it is necessary to update the jump target in eax by using the load effective address (LEA) instruction with eax+4 as base offset. This ensures that the indirect jump skips the label.

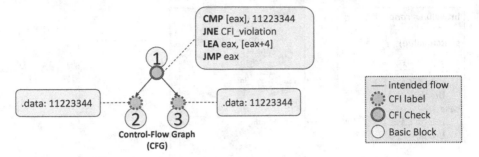

Fig. 3.3 CFI indirect jump check

3.1.2 CFI for Indirect Calls

In general, indirect call instructions are emitted by commodity compilers for (1) function calls through function pointers, (2) callbacks, and (3) C++ virtual functions. As for indirect jumps, indirect calls on x86 can either take their target address from a processor register, or directly from memory.

In the remainder of this section, we briefly describe the usage and exploitation of indirect call instructions for the invocation of C++ virtual functions. We do so, because C++ virtual table hijacking belongs to one of the most common exploitation techniques to instantiate a runtime attack.

Virtual functions support the concept of polymorphism in object-oriented languages. A prominent example to demonstrate the usefulness of virtual functions is as follows [19]: a base class shape contains a generic method *draw()* and declares it as virtual. This allows child classes such as rectangle and oval to define the same method *draw()* and implement a specific *draw()* method based on the shape's type. In C++, every class that contains virtual functions gets associated to a virtual table (vtable), where the vtable contains pointers to virtual functions. At runtime, a vtable is accessed through a vtable pointer which is stored in the object's data structure. The vtable itself typically resides in read-only memory. Hence, an adversary cannot directly compromise the integrity of the vtable to launch a runtime exploit. On the other hand, the vtable pointer resides in writable memory and is thereby subject to runtime exploits that inject a fake vtable and alter the vtable pointer to point to the injected fake vtable [49]. The next time the compromised program issues a virtual call, it will de-reference the overwritten vtable pointer and redirect the execution to the address stored in the fake vtable.

The so-called use-after-free vulnerabilities are a well-known entry point to instantiate vtable hijacking attacks [5]. The main idea of this attack technique is to exploit a dangling pointer that points to freed memory. In detail the workflow is as follows: a C++ application creates a new object of class shape. This leads to the allocation of a pointer that references the data structure of shape. In this data structure resides the vtable pointer that points to the vtable of shape. At a later time in program execution, the object is de-allocated. However, since C++ does not enforce automatic garbage collection, the pointer to the freed shape object is still intact. Given a buffer overflow vulnerability, the adversary can inject a fake vtable and overwrite the vtable pointer of the freed shape object to point to the fake vtable. Hence, making a virtual call through the dangled pointer of the freed object leads to arbitrary code execution.

Control-flow validation for indirect calls is performed as for indirect jumps: CFI assigns unique labels to valid call targets, and instruments indirect call instructions (as shown for indirect jumps in Fig. 3.3) so that they can only target a valid call site.

3.1.3 CFI for Function Returns

As we already described in Sect. 2.5, return instructions transfer control to the address located at the top of the stack. Hence, an adversary can potentially overwrite the original return address to perform a code-reuse attack.

Enforcing a label-based CFI approach on return instructions is challenging due to the fact that a single subroutine can be invoked from diverse call sites, or a single indirect function call may target multiple subroutines. The resulting CFG for both cases is shown in Fig. 3.4.

A CFI label-based approach according to the scheme presented by Abadi et al. [2, 4] will eventually lead to coarse-grained protection as a single label needs to be emitted for different call sites. Consider for this the scenario shown in Fig. 3.4a: the nodes n_A to n_Z all terminate with a function call instruction that redirects execution to the subroutine at node n_1. The exit of n_1—implemented as a return instruction—targets the call sites $n_{A'}$ to $n_{Z'}$ depending on which node has called the function, e.g.,

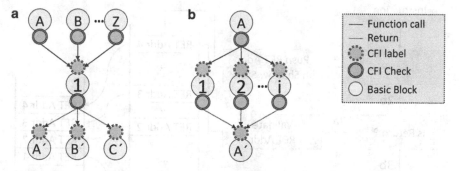

Fig. 3.4 Static label-based CFI checks for function returns. (**a**) Multiple function calls to a single subroutine; (**b**) Single indirect function call to multiple subroutines

if the function call originated from n_A then the return should target $n_{A'}$. However, since a label-based CFI approach is not aware of the runtime state of the program, it needs to emit a generic label for all call sites $n_{A'}$ to $n_{Z'}$ thereby giving an adversary the possibility to hijack the control-flow, e.g., $n_A \rightarrow n_1 \rightarrow n_{Z'}$.

In a similar vein, the scenario shown in Fig. 3.4b leads to coarse-grained CFI protection: an indirect function call at node n_A may potentially target many subroutines n_1 to n_i. Obviously, all the function returns at nodes n_1 to n_i need to redirect the control-flow to the call site at node $n_{A'}$. Hence, they all need to check against the same label, namely the label emitted at node $n_{A'}$. If there is any other node in the program that can also target one of the subroutines n_1 to n_i then its corresponding call site needs to be assigned the same label as the one already emitted at $n_{A'}$. In other words, if there is a node n_B that calls n_1 then the call site at node $n_{B'}$ is assigned the same label as $n_{A'}$. Consequently, all calling nodes from n_1 to n_i will be able to target $n_{B'}$ although n_1 is the only node that can be called by n_B.

Hence, a static CFI approach for function returns will probably lead to coarse-grained CFI enforcement where only one generic label is assigned to all call sites [2, 4]. To remedy this situation, Abadi et al. [2, 4] suggest to leverage a shadow stack [17, 28] to allow fine-grained integrity checks for return addresses.

Figure 3.5 depicts the main principle of a shadow stack: at runtime, every call and return instruction is instrumented. Whenever the program issues a call instruction the return address it pushes onto the stack is copied to a dedicated memory area called the shadow stack. Upon function return, we simply need to validate whether the return address the program attempts to use equals the one that is maintained on the shadow stack. This ensures that a return always targets its original caller even when the subroutine is frequently invoked by diverse function calls.

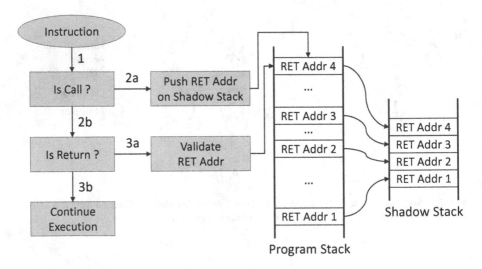

Fig. 3.5 Main principle of shadow stack (return address stack)

In order to prevent an attacker from tampering with the shadow stack, Abadi et al. [2] leverage memory segmentation which is available on x86-based systems. Alternatively, one could only allow call and return instructions to access the shadow stack using software fault isolation techniques [57].

Although the shadow stack approach allows fine-grained CFI for return instructions, it introduces several practical problems. Foremost, the performance overhead is significant due to the fact that one needs to instrument direct call instructions which occur frequently during program execution. Further, the CFI check needs to load and compare two addresses (one from the program stack and one from the shadow stack). Moreover, certain programming constructs violate the assumption that a return always needs to target its original caller. Famous examples are setjmp/longjmp, C++ exceptions which rewrite return addresses, or position-independent code that exploits call instructions to locate the current value of the program counter. Lastly, one needs to keep a shadow stack for each execution thread.

3.2 Practical CFI Implementations

CFI has been proposed as a general and fine-grained defense approach to thwart code-reuse attacks. As we described above, it derives the application's CFG prior to execution to determine the valid set of branch targets for indirect jumps and calls. At runtime, it performs control-flow checks based on the derived set of valid targets and the shadow stack which contains valid return addresses a function is allowed to return to. Although CFI requires no source code of an application, it suffers from practical limitations that impede its deployment in practice, including performance overhead of 21 %, on average [4, Sect. 5.4], when function returns are validated based on a return address (shadow) stack. To date, several CFI frameworks have been proposed that tackle the practical shortcomings of the original CFI approach. ROPecker [16] and kBouncer [45], for example, leverage the branch history table of modern x86 processors to perform a CFI check on a short history of executed branches. More recently, Zhang and Sekar [64] demonstrate a new CFI binary instrumentation approach that can be applied to commercial off-the-shelf (COTS) binaries.

However, the benefits of these practical CFI schemes come at the price of relaxing the original CFI policy. Abstractly speaking, these so-called coarse-grained CFI schemes allow for CFG relaxations that contain dozens of more legal execution paths than would be allowed under the approach first suggested by Abadi et al. [4]. The most notable difference is that the coarse-grained CFI policy for return instructions only validates if the return address points to an instruction that follows after a call instruction. In contrast, Abadi et al.'s [4] policy for fine-grained CFI ensures that the return address points to the original caller of a function (based on a shadow stack).

In the following, we revisit the assumption that coarse-grained CFI offers an effective defense against return-oriented programming. For this, we conduct a security analysis of the recently proposed CFI solutions including kBouncer [45], ROPecker [16], CFI for COTS binaries [64], ROPGuard [29], and Microsofts' EMET tool [40]. In particular, we derive a combined CFI policy that takes for each indirect branch class (i.e., return, indirect jump, indirect call) and behavioral-based heuristics (e.g., the number of instructions executed between two indirect branches), the most restrictive setting among these policies. Afterwards, we use the combined CFI policy and a weak adversary having access to only a *single*—and common used system library—to realize a Turing-complete gadget set. This gadget set can be leveraged to harden existing real-world exploits so that they bypass coarse-grained CFI protections.

3.2.1 CFI Policies

Table 3.1 summarizes the five CFI policies we use throughout this chapter to analyze the effectiveness of practical CFI schemes. Specifically, we distinguish between three types of policies, namely ① policies used for indirect branch instructions, ② general CFI heuristics that do not provide well-founded control-flow checks but instead try to capture general machine state patterns of return-oriented attacks, and ③ a policy class that covers the time CFI checks are enforced.

This categorization covers the most important aspects of CFI-based defenses suggested to date. In particular, they cover polices for each indirect branch the processor supports since all control-flow attacks (including code-reuse) require exploiting indirect branches. Second, heuristics are used by several coarse-grained CFI approaches (e.g., [29, 45]) to allow more relaxed CFI policies for indirect branches. Finally, the time-of-check policy is an important aspect because it states at which execution state return-oriented attacks can be detected. We elaborate further on each of these categories below.

①—**Indirect Branches** Recall that the goal of CFI is to validate the control-flow path taken at *indirect* branches, i.e., at those control-flow instructions that take the target address from either a processor register or from a data memory area. The indirect branch instructions present on the x86 platform are indirect calls, indirect jumps, and returns. Since CFI solutions apply different policies for each

Table 3.1 Core CFI policies to validate practical CFI schemes

Category	Policy	x86 Example	Description
①	CFI_{RET}	RET	Returns
	CFI_{JMP}	JMP reg|mem	Indirect jumps
	CFI_{CALL}	CALL reg|mem	Indirect calls
②	CFI_{HEU}		Heuristics
③	CFI_{TOC}		Time of CFI check

type of indirect branch, it is only natural that there are three CFI policies in this category, denoted as CFI_{CALL} (indirect function calls), CFI_{JMP} (indirect jumps), CFI_{RET} (function returns).

②—**Behavior-Based Heuristics (HEU)** Apart from enforcing specific policies on indirect branch instructions, CFI solutions can also validate other program behavior to detect return-oriented programming attacks. One prominent example is the number of instructions executed between two consecutive indirect branches. The expectation is that the number of such instructions will be low (compared to ordinary execution) because return-oriented programming attacks invoke a chain of short code sequences each terminating in an indirect branch instruction.

③—**Time of CFI Check (TOC)** Abadi et al. [4] argued that a CFI validation routine should be invoked whenever the program issues an indirect branch instruction. In practice, however, doing so induces significant performance overhead. For that reason, some of the more recent CFI approaches reduce the number of runtime checks, and only enforce CFI validation at critical program states, e.g., before a system or API call.

Next, we turn our attention to the specifics of how these policies are implemented in recent CFI mechanisms.

3.2.1.1 kBouncer

The approach of Pappas et al. [45], called kBouncer, deploys techniques that fall in each of the aforementioned categories. Under category ①, kBouncer leverages the x86-model register set called last branch record (LBR). The LBR provides a register set that holds the last 16 branches the processor has executed. Each branch is stored as a pair consisting of its source and target address. kBouncer performs CFI validation on the LBR entries whenever a Windows API call is invoked. Its promise resides in the fact that these checks induce almost no performance overhead, and can be directly applied to existing software programs.

With respect to its policy for returns, kBouncer identifies those LBR entries whose source address belongs to a return instruction. For these entries, kBouncer checks whether the target address (i.e., the return address) points to a *call-preceded* instruction. A call-preceded instruction is any instruction in the address space of the application that follows a call instruction. Internally, kBouncer disassembles a few bytes before the target address and terminates the process if it fails to find a call instruction.

While kBouncer does not enforce any CFI check on indirect calls and jumps, Pappas et al. [45] propose behavioral-based heuristics (category ②) to mitigate return-oriented attacks. In particular, the number of instructions executed between consecutive indirect branches (i.e., "the sequence length") is checked, and a limit is placed on the number of sequences that can be executed in a row.

A key observation by Pappas et al. [45] is that even though pure code-reuse payloads can perform Turing-complete computation, in actual exploits they will ultimately need to interact with the operating system to perform a meaningful task. Hence, as a time-of-CFI check policy (category ③) kBouncer instruments and places hooks at the entry of a WinAPI function.

3.2.1.2 ROPGuard and Microsoft EMET

Similar to kBouncer, the approach suggested by Fratric [29], called ROPGuard, performs CFI validation when a critical Windows function is called. However, ROPGuard and its implementation in Microsoft EMET [8] differ from kBouncer with respect to the CFI policies. One difference is that kBouncer checks the indirect branches executed in the past, while ROPGuard only checks the current return address of the critical function, and for future execution of gadgets.

First, with respect to policies under category ①, upon entering a critical function, ROPGuard validates whether the return address of that critical function points to a call-preceded instruction. Hence, it prevents an adversary from using an instruction sequence terminating in a return instruction to invoke the critical Windows function. In addition, ROPGuard checks if the memory word before the return address is the start address of the critical function. This would indicate that the function has been entered via a return instruction. ROPGuard also inspects the stack and predicts future execution to identify gadgets. Specifically, it walks the stack to find return addresses. If any of these return addresses points to a non-call-preceded instruction, the program is terminated.

ROPGuard's only heuristic under category ② is for validating that the stack pointer does not point to a memory location beyond the stack boundaries. While doing so prevents return-oriented payload execution on the heap, it does not prevent traditional stack-based return-oriented attacks.

3.2.1.3 ROPecker

ROPecker is a Linux-based approach suggested by Cheng et al. [16] that also leverages the LBR register set to detect past execution of gadgets. Moreover, it speculatively emulates the future program execution to detect gadgets that will be invoked in the near future. To accomplish this, a static offline phase is required to generate a database of all possible instruction sequences. To limit false positives, Cheng et al. [16] suggest that only code sequences that terminate after at most n instructions in an indirect branch should be recorded.

For its policies in category ①, ROPecker inspects each LBR entry to identify indirect branches that have redirected the control-flow to a gadget. This decision is based on the gadget database that ROPecker derived in the static analysis phase. ROPecker also inspects the program stack to predict future execution of gadgets. There is no direct policy check for indirect branches, but instead, possible gadgets are detected via a heuristic. More specifically, the robustness of its behavioral-based heuristic (category ②) completely hinges on the assumption that instruction sequences will be short and that there will always be a chain of at least some threshold number of consecutive instruction sequences.

Lastly, its TOC policy (category ③) is triggered whenever the program execution leaves a sliding window of two memory pages. Specifically, ROPecker sets all memory code pages to non-executable except (1) the page where program execution is currently performed on, and (2) the most previously executed page. When the program aims to execute code from a non-executable page, ROPecker adjusts the sliding and performs CFI validation. In addition, ROPecker hooks into some critical Linux functions. Before executing those functions, CFI validation is enforced as well.

3.2.1.4 CFI for COTS Binaries

Most closely related to the original CFI work by Abadi et al. [4] is the proposal of Zhang and Sekar [64] which suggests an approach for commercial-off-the-shelf (COTS) binaries based on a static binary rewriting approach, but without requiring debug symbols or relocation information of the target application. The CFI checks are directly incorporated into the application binary. To do so, the binary is disassembled using the Linux disassembler objdump. However, since that disassembler uses a simple linear sweep disassembly algorithm, Zhang and Sekar [64] suggest several error correction methods to ensure correct disassembly. Moreover, potential candidates of indirect control-flow target addresses are collected and recorded. These addresses comprise possible return addresses (i.e., call-preceded instructions), constant code pointers (including memory locations of pointers to external library calls), and computed code pointers (used for instance in switch-case statements). Afterwards, all indirect branch instructions are instrumented by means of a jump to a CFI validation routine.

Like the aforementioned works, the approach of Zhang and Sekar [64] checks whether a return or an indirect jump targets a call-preceded instruction. Furthermore, it also allows returns and indirect jumps to target any of the constant and computed code pointers, as well as exception handling addresses. Hence, the CFI policy for returns is not as strict as in kBouncer, where only call-preceded instructions are allowed. On the other hand, their approach deploys a CFI policy for indirect jumps, which is largely unmonitored in the other approaches. However, it does not deploy any behavioral-based heuristics (category ②).

Lastly, CFI validation (category ③) is performed whenever an indirect branch instruction is executed. Hence, it has the highest frequency of CFI validation invocation among all discussed CFI approaches.

Similar CFI policies are also enforced by CCFIR (compact CFI and randomization) [65]. In contrast to CFI for COTS binaries, all control-flow targets for indirect branches are collected and randomly allocated on a so-called springboard section. Indirect branches are only allowed to use control-flow targets contained in that springboard section. Specifically, CCFIR enforces that returns target a call-preceded instruction, and indirect calls and jumps target a previously collected function pointer. Although the randomization of control-flow targets in the springboard section adds an additional layer of security, it is not directly relevant for our analysis. Recall that memory disclosure attacks can reveal the content of the entire springboard section [55]. The CFI policies enforced by CCFIR are in principle covered by CFI for COTS binaries. However, there is one noteworthy policy addition: CCFIR denies indirect calls and jumps to target pre-defined sensitive functions (e.g., *VirtualProtect*). However, as shown by Göktas et al. [31] there are sufficient direct calls to sensitive functions in Windows libraries which an adversary can exploit to legitimately transfer control to a sensitive function.

The approach of Zhang and Sekar [64] is most similar to Abadi et al.'s [4] original proposal in that it enforces CFI policies each time an indirect branch is invoked. However, to achieve better performance and to support COTS binaries, it deploys less fine-grained CFI policies.

3.2.2 Deriving a Combined Control-Flow Integrity Policy

In the analysis that follows, we endeavor to have the best possible protections offered by the aforementioned CFI mechanisms in place at the time of our evaluation. Therefore, the combined CFI policy (see Table 3.2) selects the most restrictive setting for each policy. Nevertheless, despite this combined CFI policy, we then show that one can still circumvent these coarse-grained CFI solutions, construct Turing-complete return-oriented programming attacks (under realistic assumptions), and launch real-world exploits.

At this point, we believe it is prudent to comment on the parameter choices: one might argue that the prerequisite thresholds could be adjusted to make code-reuse attacks more difficult. To that end, we note that Pappas et al. [45] performed an extensive analysis to arrive at the best range of thresholds for the recommended number of consecutive short sequences (s) with a given sequence length of $n <= 20$. Their analysis reveals that adjusting the thresholds for s beyond their recommended values is hardly realistic: when every function call was instrumented, 975 false positives were recorded for $s <= 8$. An alternative is to increase the sequence length n (e.g., setting it to $n <= 40$). Doing so would require an adversary to find a long sequence of 40 instructions after each seventh short sequence (for $s <= 7$). However, increasing the threshold for the sequence length will only exacerbate the false positive issue.

3.2.3 Turing-Complete Gadget Set

We now explore whether or not it is possible to derive a Turing-complete gadget set even when all coarse-grained CFI protections are enforced.

Table 3.2 Policy comparison of coarse-grained CFI solutions

Control-flow integrity (CFI) Policies	CFI for COTS [64]	kBouncer [45]	ROPecker [16]	ROPGuard [29]	EMET 4.1 [40]	Combined policy
CFI_{RET} : destination has to be call-preceded	✓	✓	○	✓	✓	✓
CFI_{RET} : destination can be taken from a code pointer	✓	✗	○	✗	✗	✗
CFI_{JMP} : destination has to be call-preceded	✓	○	○	○	○	✓
CFI_{JMP} : destination can be taken from a code pointer	✓	○	○	○	○	✓
CFI_{CALL}: destination can be taken from an exported symbol	✓	○	○	○	○	✓
CFI_{CALL}: destination can be taken from a code pointer	✓	○	○	○	○	✓
CFI_{HEU} : allow only s consecutive short sequences,	○	$s <= 7$	$s <= 10$	○	○	$s <= 7$
CFI_{HEU} : where *short* is defined as n instructions	○	$n <= 20$	$n <= 6$	○	○	$n <= 20$
CFI_{TOC} : check at every indirect branch	✓	○	○	○	○	Indirect branch
CFI_{TOC} : check at critical API functions or system calls	○	✓	✓	✓	✓	✓
CFI_{TOC} : check when leaving sliding code window	○	○	✓	○	○	○

✓ indicates that the CFI policy is applied and enforced. ✗ means that the CFI policy is prohibited (corresponding execution flows would lead to an attack alarm). ○ indicates that the CFI policy is not applied/enforced. The combined policy takes the most restrictive setting for each CFI policy

Assumptions To be as pragmatic as possible, we assume that the adversary can only leverage the presence of a single shared library to derive the gadget set. This is a very stringent requirement since modern programs typically link to dozens of libraries. Note also that we are not concerned with circumventing other runtime protection mechanisms such as ASLR or stack canaries. The reason is that coarse-grained CFI protection approaches do not rely on the presence of other defenses to mitigate against code-reuse attacks.

Methodology and Outline A Turing-complete gadget set typically includes gadgets that implement a memory load, a memory store, and a conditional branch. However, since it would be very cumbersome to implement an exploit based on only these three gadget types, a Turing-complete return-oriented programming attacks typically also include gadgets for data processing, arithmetic and logical operations, and system call and function call gadgets. Specifically, we analyze `kernel32.dll` (on x86 Windows 7 SP1), a 848kb system library that exposes Windows API functions and is by default linked to nearly every major Windows process (e.g., Adobe Reader, IE, Firefox, MS Office). To facilitate the gadget finding process, we developed a static analysis script that outputs all call-preceded sequences ending in an indirect branch. We also developed a sequence filter that allows us to check for sequences containing a specific register, instruction, or memory operand. An excerpt of the Turing-complete gadget set that we constructed is shown in Table 3.1. These gadgets do not violate coarse-grained CFI policies as they all include sequences that start with a call-preceded instruction. In the following, we briefly describe these gadgets. Subsequently, we present a new gadget that allows an attacker to undermine behavioral-based heuristics.

Loading Registers Load gadgets are leveraged in nearly every return-oriented programming exploit to load a value from the stack into a CPU register. Recall that x86 provides six general-purpose registers (`eax`, `ebx`, `ecx`, `edx`, `esi`, `edi`), a base/frame pointer register (`ebp`), the stack pointer (`esp`), and the instruction pointer (`eip`). All registers can be directly accessed (read and write) by assembler instructions except the `eip` which is only indirectly influenced by dedicated branch instructions such as `RET`, `CALL`, and `JMP`.

Typically, stack loading is achieved on x86 via the `POP` instruction. The call-preceded load gadgets we identified in `kernel32.dll` are summarized in Table 3.3. Except for the `ebp` register, all gadgets induce some side-effect, i.e., they also affect other registers. However, notice that the sequence for `esi`, `edi`, and `ecx` only modifies the base pointer (`ebp`). Because traditionally `ebp` holds the base pointer and no data, and ordinary programs can be compiled without using a base pointer, `ebp` can be leveraged as an *intermediate register*. The astute reader would have noticed that the sequences for `edi` and `ecx` modify the stack pointer as well through the `LEAVE` instruction, where `LEAVE` behaves as `MOV esp,ebp; POP ebp`. However, we can handle this side-effect, since the stack pointer receives the value from the intermediate register `ebp`. Hence, one first invokes the load gadget for `ebp` and loads the desired stack pointer value, and afterwards call the sequence for `edi/ecx`.

Table 3.3 Excerpt of Turing-complete gadget set

Type	CALL-preceded sequence (ending in a RET instruction)
LOAD reg	`EBP :=` `pop ebp`
	`ESI :=` `pop esi; pop ebp`
	`EDI :=` `pop edi; leave`
	`ECX :=` `pop ecx; leave`
	`EBX :=` `pop edi; pop esi; pop ebx; pop ebp`
	`EAX :=` `mov eax,edi; pop edi; leave`
	`EDX :=` `mov eax,[ebp-8]; mov edx,[ebp-4];`
	`pop edi; leave`
Load mem	`EAX :=` `mov eax,[ebp+8]; pop ebp`
Store mem	`EAX :=` `mov [esi],eax; xor eax,eax; pop esi; pop ebp`
	`ESI :=` `mov [ebp-20h],esi`
	`EDI :=` `mov [ebp-20h],edi`
Arithmetic	`SUB :` `sub eax,esi; pop esi; pop ebp`
Logical	`XOR :` `xor eax,edi; pop edi; pop esi; pop ebp`
Branch	`UB1 :` `leave`
	`UB2 :` `add esp,0Ch; pop ebp`
Cond. load	`EAX :=` `neg eax; sbb eax,eax; and eax,[ebp-4]; leave`

More challenges arise when loading the general-purpose registers `eax`, `ebx`, and `edx`. While `ebx` can be loaded with side-effects, there are no useful stack pop sequences for `eax` and `edx`. This is not surprising given the fact that we must use call-preceded sequences. Typically, these sequences are found in function epilogues, where a function epilogue is responsible for resetting the caller-saved registers (`esi`, `edi`, `epb`). We alleviate the side-effects for `ebx` by loading all the caller-saved registers from the stack. For `eax` and `edx`, data movement gadgets can be used.

Memory Load and Store In our target library, we discovered load gadgets that use `eax` as the destination register. The specific load gadget shown in Table 3.3 loads a value from memory pointed to by `[ebp+8]`. Hence, the adversary is required to correctly set the target address of the memory load operation in `ebp` via the load register gadget.

We also identified a corresponding memory store gadget on `eax`. The shown gadget stores `eax` at the address provided by register `esi`, which needs to be initialized by a load register gadget beforehand. The gadget has no side-effects since it resets `eax` (which was stored earlier) and loads new values from the stack into `esi` (which held the target address) and `ebp` (our intermediate register).

Given a memory store gadget for `eax` and the fact that we have already identified load register gadgets for each register, it is sufficient to use the same memory load on `eax` to load any other register. Finally, there exist convenient memory store gadgets for `esi` and `edi` only requiring `ebp` to hold the target address of the store operation.

Arithmetic and Logical Gadgets For arithmetic operations, one can utilize the sequence containing the x86 SUB instruction shown in Table 3.3. This instruction takes the operands from eax and esi and stores the result of the subtraction into eax. Both operands can be loaded by using the load register gadgets. The same gadget can be used to perform an addition: one only needs to load the two's complement into esi. Based on addition and subtraction, we can realize multiplication and division as well. Logical gadgets are not as commonplace. There is, however, a XOR gadget that takes its operands from eax and edi.

Branch Gadgets Note that branching in return-oriented programming attacks is realized by modifying the stack pointer rather than the instruction pointer [53]. In general, we can distinguish two different types of branches: unconditional and conditional branches. kernel32.dll, for example, offers two variants for an unconditional branch gadget (see Table 3.3). The first uses the LEAVE instruction to load the stack pointer (esp) with a new address that has been loaded before into the intermediate register ebp. The second variant implements the unconditional branch by adding a constant offset to esp.

Conditional branch gadgets change the stack pointer iff a particular condition holds. Because load, store, and arithmetic/logic computation can be conveniently done for eax, we could place the conditional in this register. Unfortunately, because a direct load of esp (that depended on the value of eax) was not readily available, we constructed the conditional branch in three steps requiring the invocation of only four instruction sequences.

First, we use the conditional branch gadget (see Table 3.3) to either load 0 or a prepared value into eax. In this sequence NEG eax computes the two's complement and, more importantly, sets the carry flag to zero if and only if eax was zero beforehand. This is nicely used by the subsequent SBB instruction, which subtracts the register from itself, always yielding zero, but additionally subtracting an extra one if the carry flag is set. Because subtracting one from zero gives 0xFFFFFFFF, the next AND instruction masks either none or all the bits. Hence, the result in eax will be exactly the contents of [ebp-4] if eax was zero, or zero otherwise. In fact, we found 16 sequences in kernel32.dll that follow the same pattern and could have been leveraged for a conditional branch gadget.

We then use the SUB gadget to subtract esi from eax so that the latter holds the branch offset for esp. Finally, we move eax into esp using the stack as temporary storage. The store gadget will store the branch offset on the stack, where POP ebp followed by the unconditional Branch 1 gadget loads it into esp.

3.2.4   Long-NOP Gadget

There are several other gadget types that are often used in real-world code-reuse attacks. For instance, modern exploits usually invoke several critical API functions to perform malicious actions, e.g., launching a malicious executable by invoking the Windows API *WinExec( )*. Calling such functions within a return-oriented programming attack requires a function call gadget. It is also useful to have gadgets that allow one to conveniently write a NULL word to memory or a stack pivot gadget [67] which is used by return-oriented attacks exploiting heap overflows. All these gadgets can be constructed using call-preceded sequences from kernel32.dll [24]. However, in order to undermine coarse-grained CFI one still needs bypass behavioral-based heuristics.

In the remainder of this subsection, we demonstrate a generic method for circumventing the behavioral-based heuristics of the Combined CFI Policy, using a new gadget type coined long-NOP. This gadget contains a long sequence of instructions which do not break the semantics of an arbitrary return-oriented programming chain.

To identify possible sequences for this gadget type, we let our sequence finder filter those call-preceded sequences that contain more than 20 instructions. To ensure that the long sequence does not break the semantics of the return-oriented programming chain, we further reduced the set of sequences to those that (1) contain many memory write instructions and (2) make use of only a small set of registers. While the latter requirement is obvious, the former seems counter-intuitive as it can potentially change the memory state of the process. However, if we are able to control the destination address of these memory writes, we can write arbitrary values into the data area of the process outside the memory used by our code-reuse attack.

Among the sequences that fulfill these requirements, we chose a sequence that is (abstractly) shown in Fig. 3.6. It contains 13 memory write instructions using only the registers esi and edi, and does not induce any side-effects, i.e., the content of all registers and memory area used by the code-reuse attack is preserved.

We distinguish between mandatory and optional sequences used for long-NOP. The latter sequences are only required if the content of all registers needs to be preserved. We classify them as optional, since it is very unlikely that code-reuse attacks need to operate on all registers during the entire execution phase. If all registers need to be preserved (worst-case scenario), we require six sequences before the long-NOP gadget sequence is invoked. Since all registers are preserved, we can issue in each round another sequence until all desired sequences have been executed.

Mandatory Sequences The mandatory sequences are those labeled Sequence 7 and 8 (in Fig. 3.6). Sequence 7 is used to set three registers: esi, edi, and ebp. We load in esi and edi the same address, namely DATA_ADDR, which points to an arbitrary data memory area in the address space of the application, e.g., stack, heap, or any other data segment of an executable module. Due to the RET 8 instruction, the stack pointer will be incremented by 8 more bytes leaving space for pattern values. Afterwards, our long-NOP sequence uses esi and edi to issue 13 memory writes in a small window of 36 bytes. In each round, we use the same address for DATA_ADDR, and hence, we always write the same arbitrary values in a 36 byte memory space not affecting memory used by our code-reuse attack. The long-NOP

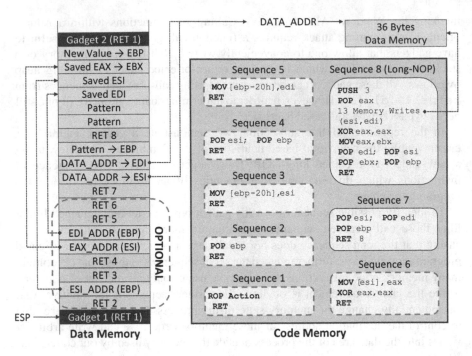

Fig. 3.6 Flow of long-NOP gadget

sequence also destroys the value of eax and loads new values via POP instructions in other registers. However, these register changes are resolved by our optional sequences discussed next.

Optional Sequences Sequence 2 to 6 are the optional sequences, and are responsible for preserving the state of all registers. Sequence 2 and 3 store the value of esi on the stack in such a way that the POP esi instruction in long-NOP resets the value accordingly. Sequence 4 to 6 store the content of eax and edi on the stack. Similar to the store for esi, the content is again re-loaded into these registers via POP instructions at the end of the long-NOP sequence. However, the content of register eax and ebx is exchanged after the long-NOP sequence since MOV eax, ebx stores ebx to eax, and the former value of eax is loaded via POP into ebx. However, one can compensate this switch by invoking the long-NOP gadget twice so that eax and ebx are exchanged again.

3.2.5 Hardening Real-World Exploits

The gadget set can be leveraged to transform existing real-world code-reuse exploits to more stealthy attacks that bypass coarse-grained CFI protection. Specifically, we transform publicly available code-reuse attacks against Adobe PDF reader [36] and the GNU mediaplayer mPlayer [12] for 32-bit Windows 7 SP1. The attacks are executed with the *Caller*, *SimExecFlow*, *StackPivot*, *LoadLib*, and *MemProt* option for ROP detection in Microsoft EMET 4.1 enabled. For the interested reader, the source code for both attacks is given in [25].

3.2.6 Other Attacks against Coarse-Grained CFI

Apart from our research, several research groups have independently investigated the security of coarse-grained CFI solutions [13, 31, 32, 34, 50]. Whereas we systematically show the construction of a Turing-complete gadget set based on a weak adversary that has only access to one standard shared Windows library, these works investigate different aspects: Göktas et al. [31] demonstrate attacks against CCFIR [65] using call-preceded gadgets to invoke sensitive functions via direct calls; Carlini and Wagner [13] and Schuster et al. [50] show flushing attacks that eliminate return-oriented programming traces before a critical function is invoked.

3.3 Research on Control-Flow Integrity

In general, control-flow integrity (CFI) provides a strong and generic defense against code-reuse attacks. However, as we have shown above, building a CFI defense that performs efficiently and at the same time comprehensively prevents code-reuse attacks is a highly challenging task. Since CFI is a very active research area at the time of writing this book, we survey the related work on CFI defenses in this section. We investigate both software-only and hardware-assisted CFI solutions.

3.3.1 Software-Only CFI Schemes

The basic principle of monitoring the control-flow of an application in order to enforce a specific security policy has been introduced by Kiriansky et al. [38] in their seminal work on program shepherding. This technique allows arbitrary restrictions to be placed on control transfers and code origins to confine a given application. Program shepherding employs dynamic binary instrumentation based on the DynamoRIO framework [10].

A more fine-grained analysis was presented by Abadi et al., who proposed control-flow integrity enforcement [2, 4]. This technique asserts the basic safety property that the control-flow of a program follows only the legitimate paths determined in advance. If an adversary hijacks the control-flow, CFI enforcement can detect this deviation and prevent the attack. In particular, Abadi et al. [1] develop a framework that is based on an abstract machine model and an instruction set to prove that CFI enforcement is sound. Davi et al. [23] show that CFI can be also applied on the ARM processor architecture to protect mobile devices against runtime exploits.

A number of binary instrumentation-based CFI schemes have appeared to tackle the performance overhead incurred by original CFI for x86 [4] and ARM [23]. We described in detail kBouncer[45], ROPGuard (Microsoft EMET) [29, 40], CFI for COTS binaries [64], ROPecker [16], and CCFIR [65] in Sect. 3.2.1. However, as we demonstrated in this chapter, even if these CFI schemes and their policies are combined with each other, they can be bypassed by advanced code-reuse attacks under weak adversarial assumptions.

The CFI schemes discussed so far employ binary instrumentation to enforce CFI. In contrast, Pewny and Holz [46] present a CFI compiler, called Control-Flow Restrictor (CFR), targeting iOS. Onarlioglu et al. [44] propose a compiler extension, called G-Free, for x86 to eliminate unintended instruction sequences of a program binary. Further, it encrypts return addresses with a random key, and constrains indirect jumps to a local function.

Control-flow locking (CFL) proposed by Bletsch et al. [9] also follows the compiler-based approach. Their technique inserts lock code before each indirect branch, and unlock code at each possible branch destination. Whereas the lock code sets a label, the unlock code checks if the correct label has been set. That is, the control-flow checks occur after the indirect branch has been taken. This allows the adversary to hijack the control-flow once. However, before the next indirect branch is executed, CFL checks whether an unlock operation has been executed. To prevent the adversary from calling a system call in-between, CFL inserts lock checks before each system call.

CFI enforcement has been also leveraged to ensure benign execution in hypervisor code. Wang and Jiang [58] introduce HyperSafe which protects x86 hypervisors by enforcing hypervisor code integrity and CFI. With respect to returns, HyperSafe only validates if the return address is within a set of possible return addresses which has been calculated offline. A more recent approach by Criswell et al. [20] explores CFI for operating system kernels.

Classic CFI schemes do not support separate compilation meaning that they do not support separate instrumentation of program modules that are later linked to one single program. As a consequence, CFI typically requires all program modules to be available at instrumentation time to assign unique labels. Niu and Tan [42] tackle this shortcoming by encoding CFG information (including labels) into dedicated tables that are consulted at runtime to perform CFI validation. In particular, MCFI merges these CFG tables when program modules need to be linked dynamically. Their tool, called MCFI, enforces fine-grained CFI based on a compiler-based approach. However, MCFI does not enforce fine-grained return address checks, i.e., a static call-graph is used to determine possible call sites for a given return instruction. In a follow-up work, Niu and Tan [43] expand MCFI protection to just-in-time (JIT) compilers. Their approach, called RockJIT, takes a hybrid approach: it enforces fine-grained CFI for the JIT compiler code, and coarse-grained CFI for code generated just-in-time.

Lastly, Prakash et al. [47] aim at enforcing system-wide CFI for kernel code and user processes. Their solution, called Total-CFI, deploys a shadow stack to enforce fine-grained checks for returns, and validates indirect jumps and calls based on a whitelist of valid targets taken from relocation tables. In its prototype implementation, Total-CFI employs dynamic translation based on QEMU to virtualize an entire guest operating system. Hence, Total-CFI incurs a large performance overhead since it requires a software emulator for the entire operating system.

3.3.2 Non-control Data Attacks

Our focus in this book are attacks and defenses against code-reuse attacks. In particular, we consider attacks that hijack the intended control-flow of an application (cf. Sect. 1.1). On the other hand, Chen et al. [15] demonstrate that non-control-data attacks are realistic and can be launched against modern applications. The main idea of these attacks is to alter application data such as user input, configuration data, user ID, or authentication data to execute privileged code without violating control-flow integrity.

Data-flow integrity (DFI) proposed by Castro et al. [14] aims at preventing non-control-data attacks. To do so, DFI derives the static data-flow graph (DFG) of an application, and inserts runtime checks to validate if read and write operations follow the legitimate data flow given in the DFG. Write Integrity Testing (WIT) proposed by Akritidis et al. [6] extends the original DFI work. It leverages interprocedural points to analysis which outputs the CFG, and computes the set of objects that can be written by each instruction in the program. Based on the result of the points to analysis, WIT assigns a color to each object and each write instruction. WIT enforces write integrity by only allowing the write operation if the originating instruction and the target object share the same color. As a second line of defense, it also enforces CFI to check if an indirect call targets a valid execution path in the CFG.

3.3.3 Inlined Reference Monitors

In general, one can classify CFI as an instantiation of an Inlined Reference Monitors (IRM). To insert an IRM into an application, a rewriter or compiler produces—based on a given security policy and the original program's binary or source code—a secured application [26]. The IRM ensures that program execution does never violate the security policy. In CFI [4], the IRM consists of CFI label checks and the shadow stack for returns to ensure that the control-flow always follows a legitimate path in the CFG. In fact, the CFG resembles the security policy.

Apart from CFI, there are several other well-known IRM schemes such as software fault isolation (SFI) [57]. Although their goals slightly differ from CFI, they share many similarities to CFI. Moreover, many SFI schemes are combined with some form of CFI to ensure that the IRM is not compromised by runtime exploits. In the following, we provide a brief overview of SFI schemes.

The basic idea of SFI is to isolate code and data of an untrusted module in a separate fault domain [57]. Afterwards, the untrusted module is instrumented to ensure that the code cannot jump or reference data beyond its fault domain. The original SFI proposal targeted RISC architectures, and is not applicable to architectures that feature variable-length instructions. McCamant and Morrisett [39] tackle this shortcoming and presented a SFI scheme, called PittSFIeld, for the CISC-based architecture x86. PittSFIeld aligns branch instructions to a 16-Byte boundary. To do so, it emits NOP instructions to ensure that all possible branch targets are aligned to 16 Bytes. NativeClient (NaCl) [52, 60] builds upon SFI and enables a sandboxed environment for native code plugins in web browsers.

Abadi et al. [3] propose XFI as an extension to their original x86-based CFI scheme [4]. In particular, XFI allows enforcement of fine-grained memory access control rules. For this, it employs a XFI rewriter and verifier to insert software guards that perform runtime checks on control-flow and memory access.

Zeng et al. [62] showed that CFI combined with static analysis enables the enforcement of efficient data sandboxing. In particular, the presented scheme provides confidentiality of critical memory regions by constraining memory reads to uncritical data regions. This is achieved by placing guard zones before and after the uncritical data area. The solution has been implemented in the LLVM compiler infrastructure (similar to the NaCl compiler [52, 60]) and targets x86 platforms.

The aforementioned schemes have a practical limitation: they target a specific hardware architecture and porting them to other architectures involves significant effort. To address this limitation, Zeng et al. [61] propose Strato which is a framework that enables IRM implementations at the compiler intermediate representation (IR) level.

Although CFI offers a viable defense to protect IRM schemes, it typically does not allow separate compilation. Niu and Tan [41] tackles this limitation by dividing code into chunks and restricting indirect branches to only target the first instruction of a chunk. The boundaries of code chunks are stored in the module's chunk table. The tool, called Monitor Integrity Protection (MIP), maintains a bitmap per chunk table, and supports static as well as dynamic combination of program modules by merging chunk tables on-demand.

3.3.4 Hardware-Assisted CFI Schemes

Several approaches leveraged (or introduced new) hardware-based mechanisms to mitigate runtime exploits. For instance, kBouncer and ROPecker use the Last Branch Recording (LBR) history table of recent processors [16, 45]. They add hooks into API call sites, and once these are triggered at runtime, validate the LBR entries based on a CFI policy.

Similarly, Xia et al. [59] use performance counters and the Branch Trace Store (BTS) to detect control-flow deviations. Zhang et al. [63] aim at detecting program execution anomalies based on a new hardware architecture that validates all branch instructions. However, both approaches require an offline training phase [59, 63], and assume a precise and static CFG.

Budiu et al. [11] present a hardware-based CFI design for the Alpha Simulator. In their work, new hardware CFI instructions are introduced to enforce label checks on each indirect branch. For this, each branch target is annotated with a label instruction (CFILABEL L), and every indirect branch is replaced by a corresponding CFI instruction, e.g., JMPC reg, L. The latter CFI instruction jumps to the address specified in reg and at the same time sets a label L in a dedicated (new) CFI register. After the indirect branch has been executed, the processor changes state such that CFILABEL is the only permissible next instruction.

Davi et al. [7] introduce CFI instructions that allow for efficient checking of return instructions. They track call chains by maintaining label state in an on-chip memory, and constrain function returns to only target a call site of currently executing function. Branch regulation as proposed by Kayaalp et al. [37] requires identifying function bounds and a shadow stack to enforce fine-grained CFI.

Francillon et al. [27] introduce an embedded microprocessor that includes memory access control for the stack, which is split into data-only and call/return addresses-only parts. The processor enforces access control that does not allow to overwrite the call/return stack with arbitrary data. This effectively prevents stack-based return-oriented attacks.

Frantzen and Shuey [28] propose a hardware-facilitated solution, called Stack-Ghost, which targets SPARC-based systems. It leverages stack cookies that are XORed with return addresses at function entry, and XORed again upon function return. The design of StackGhost also includes a return address stack (i.e., shadow stack).

3.3.5 Backward-Edge CFI Schemes

Several CFI schemes focus exclusively on enforcing integrity checks for return instructions. These backward-edge CFI schemes aim at mitigating conventional return-oriented programming attacks (cf. Sect. 2.5.2).

Chiueh and Hsu [17] present a compiler-based implementation of a shadow stack. Several approaches aim to detect malicious change of return addresses by using instrumentation techniques without requiring source code. Gupta et al. [33] and Chiueh and Prasad [18] rewrite function prologue and epilogue instructions to incorporate a return address check on each function return. However, both approaches are not able to detect return-oriented attacks that use unintended instruction sequences, because they only instrument intended function epilogues.

In contrast, TRUSS (Transparent Runtime Shadow Stack) [54] and ROPde-fender [22] are based on just-in-time based instrumentation. These approaches leverage a shadow stack to perform integrity checks for return addresses. Due to just-in-time instrumentation, TRUSS and ROPdefender are able to detect the execution of unintended sequences.

Recently, Dang et al. [21] review several shadow stack-based CFI schemes and demonstrate that performance can be increased by leveraging a parallel shadow stack. However, the parallel stack resides in the address space of the target application.

3.3.6   Forward-Edge CFI Schemes

As there exist CFI schemes that focus on return instructions (backward-edge CFI), there exist schemes protecting indirect jumps and calls (forward-edge CFI). For instance, the approaches of Tice et al. [56] and Jang et al. [35] focus on protecting indirect calls to virtual methods in C++. Both approaches have been implemented as a compiler extension and ensure that an adversary cannot manipulate a virtual table (vtable) pointer so that it points to an adversary-controlled (malicious) vtable.

The aforementioned approaches require the source code of the application which might not be always readily available. In order to protect binary code, a number of forward-edge CFI schemes have been presented recently [30, 48, 66]. Although these approaches require no access to source code, they are not as fine-grained as their compiler-based counterparts. A novel attack technique, called COOP (counterfeit object-oriented programming), undermines the CFI protection of these binary instrumentation-based defenses by invoking a chain of virtual methods through legitimate call sites to induce malicious program behavior [51].

3.4   Summary and Conclusion

Without question, control-flow integrity offers a strong defense against runtime exploits. Its promise lies in the fact that it provides a general defense mechanism to thwart such attacks. Unfortunately, several pragmatic issues (most notably, its relatively high performance overhead), have limited its widespread adoption.

To better tackle the trade-off between security and performance, several coarse-grained CFI solutions have been proposed. These proposals all use relaxed policies. While many advancements have been made along the way, all to often the relaxed enforcement policies significantly diminish the security afforded by Abadi et al. [4]'s seminal work. This realization is a bit troubling, and calls for a broader acceptance that we should not sacrifice security for small performance gains. Doing so simply does not raise the bar high enough to deter skillful adversaries.

References

1. Abadi, M., Budiu, M., Erlingsson, Ú., Ligatti, J.: A theory of secure control-flow. In: Proceedings of the 7th International Conference on Formal Methods and Software Engineering, ICFEM'05 (2005). URL http://dx.doi.org/10.1007/11576280_9
2. Abadi, M., Budiu, M., Erlingsson, Ú., Ligatti, J.: Control-flow integrity: principles, implementations, and applications. In: Proceedings of the 12th ACM Conference on Computer and Communications Security, CCS'05 (2005). URL http://doi.acm.org/10.1145/1102120.1102165
3. Abadi, M., Budiu, M., Erlingsson, Ú., Necula, G.C., Vrable, M.: XFI: Software guards for system address spaces. In: Proceedings of the 7th Symposium on Operating Systems Design and Implementation, OSDI'06 (2006). URL http://dl.acm.org/citation.cfm?id=1298455.1298463
4. Abadi, M., Budiu, M., Erlingsson, U., Ligatti, J.: Control-flow integrity: principles, implementations, and applications. ACM Trans. Inf. Syst. Secur. 13(1), 4:1–4:40 (2009). URL http://doi.acm.org/10.1145/1609956.1609960
5. Afek, J., Sharabani, A.: Dangling pointer: smashing the pointer for fun and profit (2007). URL https://www.blackhat.com/presentations/bh-usa-07/Afek/Whitepaper/bh-usa-07-afek-WP.pdf
6. Akritidis, P., Cadar, C., Raiciu, C., Costa, M., Castro, M.: Preventing memory error exploits with WIT. In: Proceedings of the 29th IEEE Symposium on Security and Privacy, SP'08 (2008). URL http://dx.doi.org/10.1109/SP.2008.30
7. Arias, O., Davi, L., Hanreich, M., Jin, Y., Koeberl, P., Paul, D., Sadeghi, A.R., Sullivan, D.: HAFIX: hardware-assisted flow integrity extension. In: Proceedings of the 52nd Design Automation Conference, DAC'15. (2015) doi: http://doi.acm.org/10.1145/2744769.2744847
8. Bachaalany, E.: Inside EMET 4.0. REcon Montreal (2013). URL http://recon.cx/2013/slides/Recon2013-Elias%20Bachaalany-Inside%20EMET%204.pdf
9. Bletsch, T., Jiang, X., Freeh, V.: Mitigating code-reuse attacks with control-flow locking. In: Proceedings of the 27th Annual Computer Security Applications Conference, ACSAC'11 (2011). URL http://doi.acm.org/10.1145/2076732.2076783
10. Bruening, D.L.: Efficient, transparent, and comprehensive runtime code manipulation. Ph.D. thesis, Massachusetts Institute of Technology (2004). URL http://groups.csail.mit.edu/cag/rio/derek-phd-thesis.pdf
11. Budiu, M., Erlingsson, U., Abadi, M.: Architectural support for software-based protection. In: Proceedings of the 1st Workshop on Architectural and System Support for Improving Software Dependability, ASID'06, pp. 42–51 (2006). URL http://doi.acm.org/10.1145/1181309.1181316
12. C4SS!0, h1ch4m: MPlayer Lite r33064 m3u buffer overflow exploit (DEP Bypass) (2011). URL http://www.exploit-db.com/exploits/17565/
13. Carlini, N., Wagner, D.: ROP is still dangerous: breaking modern defenses. In: Proceedings of the 23rd USENIX Security Symposium (2014). URL http://dl.acm.org/citation.cfm?id=2671225.2671250
14. Castro, M., Costa, M., Harris, T.: Securing software by enforcing data-flow integrity. In: Proceedings of the 7th Symposium on Operating Systems Design and Implementation, OSDI'06 (2006). URL http://dl.acm.org/citation.cfm?id=1298455.1298470
15. Chen, S., Xu, J., Sezer, E.C., Gauriar, P., Iyer, R.K.: Non-control-data attacks are realistic threats. In: Proceedings of the 14th USENIX Security Symposium (2005). URL http://dl.acm.org/citation.cfm?id=1251398.1251410
16. Cheng, Y., Zhou, Z., Miao, Y., Ding, X., Deng, R.H.: ROPecker: a generic and practical approach for defending against ROP attacks. In: Proceedings of the 21st Annual Network and Distributed System Security Symposium, NDSS'14 (2014). URL http://www.internetsociety.org/doc/ropecker-generic-and-practical-approach-defending-against-rop-attacks
17. Chiueh, T., Hsu, F.H.: RAD: A compile-time solution to buffer overflow attacks. In: Proceedings of the 21st International Conference on Distributed Computing Systems, ICDCS'01 (2001). URL http://dl.acm.org/citation.cfm?id=876878.879316

18. Chiueh, T., Prasad, M.: A binary rewriting defense against stack based overflow attacks. In: Proceedings of the 2003 USENIX Annual Technical Conference, ATC'03 (2003). URL https:// www.usenix.org/legacy/event/usenix03/tech/full_papers/prasad/prasad_html/camera.html
19. cplusplus.com: Polymorphism. URL http://www.cplusplus.com/doc/tutorial/polymorphism/
20. Criswell, J., Dautenhahn, N., Adve, V.: KCoFI: complete control-flow integrity for commodity operating system kernels. In: Proceedings of the 2014 IEEE Symposium on Security and Privacy, SP'14 (2014). URL http://dx.doi.org/10.1109/SP.2014.26
21. Dang, T.H., Maniatis, P., Wagner, D.: The performance cost of shadow stacks and stack canaries. In: Proceedings of the 10th ACM Symposium on Information, Computer and Communications Security, ASIACCS'15 (2015). URL http://doi.acm.org/10.1145/2714576. 2714635
22. Davi, L., Sadeghi, A.R., Winandy, M.: ROPdefender: a detection tool to defend against return-oriented programming attacks. In: Proceedings of the 6th ACM Symposium on Information, Computer and Communications Security, ASIACCS'11 (2011). URL http://doi.acm.org/10. 1145/1966913.1966920
23. Davi, L., Dmitrienko, A., Egele, M., Fischer, T., Holz, T., Hund, R., Nürnberger, S., Sadeghi, A.R.: MoCFI: a framework to mitigate control-flow attacks on smartphones. In: Proceedings of the 19th Annual Network and Distributed System Security Symposium, NDSS'12 (2012). URL http://www.internetsociety.org/mocfi-framework-mitigate-control-flow-attacks-smartphones
24. Davi, L., Lehmann, D., Sadeghi, A.R., Monrose, F.: Stitching the gadgets: on the ineffectiveness of coarse-grained control-flow integrity protection. In: Proceedings of the 23rd USENIX Security Symposium (2014). URL http://dl.acm.org/citation.cfm?id=2671225.2671251
25. Davi, L., Lehmann, D., Sadeghi, A.R., Monrose, F.: Stitching the gadgets: on the ineffectiveness of coarse-grained control-flow integrity protection. Technical Report TUD-CS-2014-0097, Technische Universität Darmstadt (2014). URL https://www.informatik.tu-darmstadt. de/fileadmin/user_upload/Group_TRUST/PubsPDF/techreport-stitching-gadgets.pdf
26. Erlingsson, U.: The inlined reference monitor approach to security policy enforcement. Ph.D. thesis, Cornell University (2004). URL http://www.ru.is/faculty/ulfar/thesis.pdf
27. Francillon, A., Perito, D., Castelluccia, C.: Defending embedded systems against control flow attacks. In: Proceedings of the First ACM Workshop on Secure Execution of Untrusted Code, SecuCode'09 (2009). URL http://doi.acm.org/10.1145/1655077.1655083
28. Frantzen, M., Shuey, M.: StackGhost: hardware facilitated stack protection. In: Proceedings of the 10th USENIX Security Symposium (2001). URL http://dl.acm.org/citation.cfm?id= 1251327.1251332
29. Fratric, I.: ROPGuard: runtime prevention of return-oriented programming attacks (2012). URL http://www.ieee.hr/_download/repository/Ivan_Fratric.pdf
30. Gawlik, R., Holz, T.: Towards automated integrity protection of C++ virtual function tables in binary programs. In: Proceedings of the 30th Annual Computer Security Applications Conference, ACSAC'14 (2014). URL http://doi.acm.org/10.1145/2664243.2664249
31. Göktas, E., Athanasopoulos, E., Bos, H., Portokalidis, G.: Out of control: overcoming control-flow integrity. In: Proceedings of the 35th IEEE Symposium on Security and Privacy, SP'14 (2014). URL http://dx.doi.org/10.1109/SP.2014.43
32. Göktas, E., Athanasopoulos, E., Polychronakis, M., Bos, H., Portokalidis, G.: Size does matter: why using gadget-chain length to prevent code-reuse attacks is hard. In: Proceedings of the 23rd USENIX Security Symposium (2014). URL http://dl.acm.org/citation.cfm?id=2671225. 2671252
33. Gupta, S., Pratap, P., Saran, H., Arun-Kumar, S.: Dynamic code instrumentation to detect and recover from return address corruption. In: Proceedings of the 2006 International Workshop on Dynamic Systems Analysis, WODA'06, pp. 65–72 (2006). URL http://doi.acm.org/10.1145/ 1138912.1138926
34. Jalayeri, S.: Bypassing EMET 3.5's ROP mitigations (2012). URL https://repret.wordpress. com/2012/08/08/bypassing-emet-3-5s-rop-mitigations/

35. Jang, D., Tatlock, Z., Lerner, S.: SAFEDISPATCH: securing C++ virtual calls from memory corruption attacks. In: Proceedings of the 21st Annual Network and Distributed System Security Symposium, NDSS'14 (2014). URL http://www.internetsociety.org/doc/safedispatch-securing-c-virtual-calls-memory-corruption-attacks

36. jduck: the latest Adobe exploit and session upgrading (2010). URL http://bugix-security.blogspot.de/2010/03/adobe-pdf-libtiff-working-exploitcve.html

37. Kayaalp, M., Ozsoy, M., Abu-Ghazaleh, N., Ponomarev, D.: Branch regulation: low-overhead protection from code reuse attacks. In: Proceedings of the 39th Annual International Symposium on Computer Architecture, ISCA'12 (2012). URL http://dl.acm.org/citation.cfm?id=2337159.2337171

38. Kiriansky, V., Bruening, D., Amarasinghe, S.P.: Secure execution via program shepherding. In: Proceedings of the 11th USENIX Security Symposium (2002). URL http://dl.acm.org/citation.cfm?id=647253.720293

39. McCamant, S., Morrisett, G.: Evaluating SFI for a CISC architecture. In: Proceedings of the 15th USENIX Security Symposium (2006). URL http://dl.acm.org/citation.cfm?id=1267336.1267351

40. Microsoft: enhanced Mitigation Experience Toolkit. URL https://www.microsoft.com/emet

41. Niu, B., Tan, G.: Monitor integrity protection with space efficiency and separate compilation. In: Proceedings of the 20th ACM Conference on Computer and Communications Security, CCS'13 (2013). URL http://doi.acm.org/10.1145/2508859.2516649

42. Niu, B., Tan, G.: Modular control-flow integrity. In: Proceedings of the 35th ACM SIGPLAN Conference on Programming Language Design and Implementation, PLDI'14 (2014). URL http://doi.acm.org/10.1145/2594291.2594295

43. Niu, B., Tan, G.: RockJIT: securing just-in-time compilation using modular control-flow integrity. In: Proceedings of the 21st ACM Conference on Computer and Communications Security, CCS'14 (2014). URL http://doi.acm.org/10.1145/2660267.2660281

44. Onarlioglu, K., Bilge, L., Lanzi, A., Balzarotti, D., Kirda, E.: G-Free: defeating return-oriented programming through gadget-less binaries. In: Proceedings of the 26th Annual Computer Security Applications Conference, ACSAC'10 (2010). URL http://doi.acm.org/10.1145/1920261.1920269

45. Pappas, V., Polychronakis, M., Keromytis, A.D.: Transparent ROP exploit mitigation using indirect branch tracing. In: Proceedings of the 22nd USENIX Security Symposium (2013). URL http://dl.acm.org/citation.cfm?id=2534766.2534805

46. Pewny, J., Holz, T.: Compiler-based CFI for iOS. In: Proceedings of the 29th Annual Computer Security Applications Conference, ACSAC'13 (2013). URL http://doi.acm.org/10.1145/2523649.2523674

47. Prakash, A., Yin, H., Liang, Z.: Enforcing system-wide control flow integrity for exploit detection and diagnosis. In: Proceedings of the 8th ACM Symposium on Information, Computer and Communications Security, ASIACCS'13 (2013). URL http://doi.acm.org/10.1145/2484313.2484352

48. Prakash, A., Hu, X., Yin, H.: vfGuard: strict protection for virtual function calls in COTS C++ binaries. In: Proceedings of the 22nd Annual Network and Distributed System Security Symposium, NDSS'15 (2015). URL http://www.internetsociety.org/doc/vfguard-strict-protection-virtual-function-calls-cots-c-binaries

49. rix: Smashing C++ VPTRS. Phrack Magazine 56(8) (2000). URL http://phrack.org/issues/56/8.html

50. Schuster, F., Tendyck, T., Pewny, J., Maaß, A., Steegmanns, M., Contag, M., Holz, T.: Evaluating the effectiveness of current anti-rop defenses. In: Research in Attacks, Intrusions and Defenses. Lecture Notes in Computer Science, Springer Intertnational Publishing, vol. 8688 (Springer, 2014). URL http://dx.doi.org/10.1007/978-3-319-11379-1_5

51. Schuster, F., Tendyck, T., Liebchen, C., Davi, L., Sadeghi, A.R., Holz, T.: Counterfeit object-oriented programming: on the difficulty of preventing code reuse attacks in C++ applications. In: Proceedings of the 36th IEEE Symposium on Security and Privacy, SP'15 (2015). doi=10.1109/SP.2015.51

52. Sehr, D., Muth, R., Biffle, C., Khimenko, V., Pasko, E., Schimpf, K., Yee, B., Chen, B.: Adapting software fault isolation to contemporary CPU architectures. In: Proceedings of the 19th USENIX Security Symposium (2010). URL http://dl.acm.org/citation.cfm?id=1929820. 1929822
53. Shacham, H.: The geometry of innocent flesh on the bone: Return-into-libc without function calls (on the x86). In: Proceedings of the 14th ACM Conference on Computer and Communications Security, CCS'07 (2007). URL http://doi.acm.org/10.1145/1315245.1315313
54. Sinnadurai, S., Zhao, Q., Fai Wong, W.: Transparent runtime shadow stack: protection against malicious return address modifications (2008). URL http://citeseerx.ist.psu.edu/viewdoc/summary?doi=10.1.1.120.5702s
55. Snow, K.Z., Monrose, F., Davi, L., Dmitrienko, A., Liebchen, C., Sadeghi, A.R.: Just-in-time code reuse: on the effectiveness of fine-grained address space layout randomization. In: Proceedings of the 34th IEEE Symposium on Security and Privacy, SP'13 (2013). URL http://dx.doi.org/10.1109/SP.2013.45. Received the Best Student Paper Award
56. Tice, C., Roeder, T., Collingbourne, P., Checkoway, S., Erlingsson, Ú., Lozano, L., Pike, G.: Enforcing forward-edge control-flow integrity in GCC & LLVM. In: Proceedings of the 23rd USENIX Security Symposium (2014). URL http://dl.acm.org/citation.cfm?id=2671225. 2671285
57. Wahbe, R., Lucco, S., Anderson, T.E., Graham, S.L.: Efficient software-based fault isolation. SIGOPS Oper. Syst. Rev. 27(5), 203–216 (1993). URL http://doi.acm.org/10.1145/173668. 168635
58. Wang, Z., Jiang, X.: HyperSafe: a lightweight approach to provide lifetime hypervisor control-flow integrity. In: Proceedings of the 31st IEEE Symposium on Security and Privacy, SP'10 (2010). URL http://dx.doi.org/10.1109/SP.2010.30
59. Xia, Y., Liu, Y., Chen, H., Zang, B.: CFIMon: detecting violation of control flow integrity using performance counters. In: Proceedings of the 2012 42nd Annual IEEE/IFIP International Conference on Dependable Systems and Networks, DSN'12 (2012). URL http://dl.acm.org/citation.cfm?id=2354410.2355130
60. Yee, B., Sehr, D., Dardyk, G., Chen, J.B., Muth, R., Ormandy, T., Okasaka, S., Narula, N., Fullagar, N.: Native Client: a sandbox for portable, untrusted x86 native code. In: Proceedings of the 30th IEEE Symposium on Security and Privacy, SP'09 (2009). URL http://dx.doi.org/10.1109/SP.2009.25
61. Zeng, B., Tan, G., Erlingsson, U.: Strato: a retargetable framework for low-level inlined-reference monitors. In: Proceedings of the 22nd USENIX Security Symposium (2013). URL http://dl.acm.org/citation.cfm?id=2534766.2534798
62. Zeng, B., Tan, G., Morrisett, G.: Combining control-flow integrity and static analysis for efficient and validated data sandboxing. In: Proceedings of the 18th ACM Conference on Computer and Communications Security, CCS'11 (2011). URL http://doi.acm.org/10.1145/2046707.2046713
63. Zhang, T., Zhuang, X., Pande, S., Lee, W.: Anomalous path detection with hardware support. In: Proceedings of the 2005 International Conference on Compilers, Architectures and Synthesis for Embedded Systems, CASES'05 (2005). URL http://doi.acm.org/10.1145/1086297. 1086305
64. Zhang, M., Sekar, R.: Control flow integrity for COTS binaries. In: Proceedings of the 22nd USENIX Security Symposium (2013). URL http://dl.acm.org/citation.cfm?id=2534766. 2534796
65. Zhang, C., Wei, T., Chen, Z., Duan, L., Szekeres, L., McCamant, S., Song, D., Zou, W.: Practical control flow integrity & randomization for binary executables. In: Proceedings of the 34th IEEE Symposium on Security and Privacy, SP'13 (2013). URL http://dx.doi.org/10. 1109/SP.2013.44
66. Zhang, C., Song, C., Chen, K.Z., Chen, Z., Song, D.: VTint: defending virtual function tables' integrity. In: Proceedings of the 22nd Annual Network and Distributed System Security Symposium, NDSS'15 (2015). URL http://www.internetsociety.org/doc/vtint-protecting-virtual-function-tables%E2%80%99-integrity
67. Zovi, D.D.: Practical return-oriented programming. SOURCE Boston (2010). URL http://trailofbits.files.wordpress.com/2010/04/practical-rop.pdf

Chapter 4
Building Code Randomization Defenses

4.1 Basics of Code Randomization

The idea of software diversity (or program evolution) has been introduced by
Cohen [7] in his seminal work on how to protect computer systems and their
running software programs against software exploits. The basic observation is
that an adversary typically generates an attack vector and aims to simultaneously
compromise as many systems as possible using the same attack vector (i.e., one
attack payload). To mitigate this so-called ultimate attack, Cohen proposes to
diversify a software program into multiple and different instances while each
instance still covers the entire semantics of the root software program. The goal
is to force the adversary to tailor a specific attack vector/payload for each software
instance and computer system making the attack tremendously expensive.

4.1.1 Address Space Layout Randomization

A well-accepted countermeasure against code-reuse attacks is the randomization of
the application's memory layout. The basic idea of address space layout randomization (ASLR) dates back to Forrest et al. [11], wherein a new stack memory allocator
was introduced that adds a random pad for stack objects larger than 16 Bytes. Today,
ASLR is enabled on nearly all modern operating systems such as Windows, Linux,
iOS, or Android. For the most part, current ASLR schemes randomize the base
(start) address of segments such as the stack, heap, libraries, and the executable
itself. This basic approach is depicted in Fig. 4.1, where the start address of the
program executable, its shared libraries, and data segments is relocated between
consecutive runs of the application. As a result, an adversary must guess the location
of the functions and instruction sequences needed for successful deployment of her
code-reuse attack. Hence, we define ASLR as follows.

© The Author(s) 2015   55
L. Davi, A.-R. Sadeghi, *Building Secure Defenses Against Code-Reuse Attacks*,
SpringerBriefs in Computer Science, DOI 10.1007/978-3-319-25546-0_4

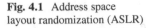

Fig. 4.1 Address space
layout randomization (ASLR)

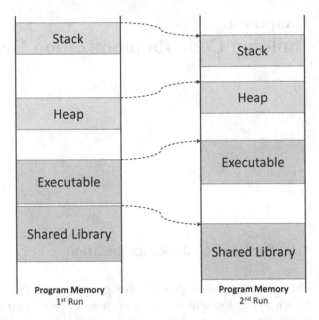

Address Space Layout Randomization (ASLR): *In order to defend against code-reuse attacks, address space layout randomization randomizes the base address of code and data segments per execution run. Hence, the memory location of code that the adversary attempts to use will reside at a random memory location.*

Unfortunately, today's ASLR realizations suffer from two main problems: first, the entropy on 32-bit systems is too low, and thus ASLR can be bypassed by means of brute-force attacks [26, 30]. The main idea of such attacks is to guess the address of a single library function residing in libc. For instance, the attacker attempts to execute the *sleep()* function to halt program execution for a pre-defined time. Recently, Bittau et al. [6] demonstrate that even 64-bit based systems—where the randomization entropy is significantly larger—can be compromised by means of brute-force attacks on code randomization. The introduced technique, denoted as BROP (blind ROP), probes on byte granularity the stack to eventually disclose gadgets based on whether the target server crashed or execution has continued. However, brute-force attacks typically only apply to server applications that do not re-randomize after a crash. Second, all ASLR solutions are vulnerable to *memory disclosure* attacks [29, 32] where the adversary gains knowledge of a single runtime address and uses that information to re-enable code-reuse in her playbook once again. We remind the reader that this is possible because ASLR only randomizes the base address of the segment meaning that the randomization offset within one segment always remains the same.

For such a memory disclosure attack, consider an application that links to the standard UNIX C library libc to invoke the *printf()* function. The adversary's goal is to mount a code-reuse attack using various gadgets from libc. At compile-time, the runtime address of *printf()* is not known as ASLR allocates libc at a randomized memory location for each run. However, the compiler will add a placeholder for the runtime address of *printf()* into a dedicated data section of the executable that is called global offset table (GOT). At application runtime, the dynamic loader will resolve and allocate the runtime address of *printf()* into the GOT either at load-time of the application or on-demand when *printf()* is called for the first time. As the GOT is readable, an adversary can learn the runtime address of *printf()*. In practice, this can be achieved by using a non-randomized gadget [13], or by exploiting a so-called format string vulnerability which allows arbitrary reads and writes in the address space of an application [14]. Given the runtime address of *printf()*, the adversary can determine the start address of libc as the offset is constant. Once the start address is known, the adversary dynamically adjusts all the pointers inside the return-oriented payload using the constant randomization offset.

4.1.2 Fine-Grained Code Randomization

As we described above, base address randomization by means of ASLR [28] cannot resist control-flow attacks that exploit a memory disclosure vulnerability beforehand. To tackle this limitation, a number of so-called fine-grained ASLR, i.e., fine-grained code randomization schemes,[1] have recently appeared in the academic literature [5, 9, 18, 24, 27, 34]. The underlying idea in these works is to randomize the code structure, for instance, by shuffling functions, basic blocks, or instructions (ideally for each program run [9, 34]).

Figure 4.2 demonstrates how fine-grained ASLR is applied to an application with three code blocks. For each execution, base address randomization ensures

Fig. 4.2 Fine-grained code randomization

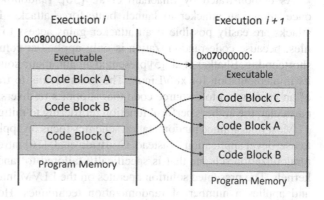

---

[1]Note that we use both terms interchangeably.

that the executable is loaded at a start address different from the previous execution. In addition, fine-grained ALSR permutes the code blocks such that an adversary can no longer deploy a code-reuse attack by disclosing a single runtime address. Obviously, changing the order of code blocks requires adjusting memory offsets used in the code blocks. For instance, if Code Block B in Fig. 4.2 issues a branch instruction to redirect execution to Code Block C, it will be necessary to adjust the branch target as Code Block C has been moved to the beginning of the executable.

In the following, we provide a selected overview on fine-grained code randomization schemes. We distinguish between compiler-based and binary instrumentation based approaches. We also refer the reader to the systematization of knowledge paper by Larsen et al. [25] that provides a detailed comparison of fine-grained code randomization schemes.

4.1.2.1   Source Code and Compiler-Based Solutions

Franz [12] and Jackson et al. [21] have explored the feasibility of a compiler-based approach for large-scale software diversity in the mobile market. The authors suggest that app store providers integrate a multicompiler (diversifier) in the code production process. This allows an app store to distribute semantically equivalent but diversified apps for mobile devices.

Jackson et al. [22] also implement and evaluate a diversity compiler for LLVM and GCC. Their randomization technique is solely based on inserting non-alignment NOP instructions allowing protection of the entire system including the kernel. To improve performance, Homescu et al. [20] apply profiling techniques to identify frequently executed code parts. For these hot code parts, Homescu et al. [20] sparsely insert NOP instructions, which yields significantly better performance. Moreover, Homescu et al. [19] explore NOP diversification for dynamically generated code. However, emitting NOP instructions does not yield a high randomization entropy, because basic block and function order remain unchanged.

As demonstrated by Shacham et al. [30], randomizing an application only once allows an attacker to launch brute-force attacks. In particular, code-reuse attacks are easily possible if an attacker gains access to the applications' binary files, because code randomization is only applied at compile-time. To tackle this shortcoming, Bhatkar et al. [5] presented an automatic source code transformer and its implementation for x86/Linux. The main idea is to transform the source code of an application to a source code that supports re-diversification for each run. In particular, the authors perform function reordering to mitigate code-reuse attacks.

Most fine-grained randomization schemes focus on applying code randomization to user-level applications. Instead, Giuffrida et al. [16] introduce a fine-grained code randomization scheme that is specifically tailored to randomize operating system kernels. The presented solution operates on the LLVM intermediate representation, and applies a number of randomization techniques. However, the approach of Giuffrida et al. [16] is best suited to microkernels, while most modern operating systems (Windows, Linux, Mac OSX) still follow a monolithic design.

In general, compiler-based solutions have the potential to provide among all software diversity approaches the highest degree of entropy due to the access to source code. However, source code is not always available in practice.

4.1.2.2   Binary Instrumentation Based Solutions

These techniques directly operate on the application binary to perform software diversity. Bhatkar et al. [4] analyze and propose enhanced randomization techniques such as code transformation and insertion of random gaps between adjacent objects. However, the authors only implemented a tool that performs base address randomization and insertion of random gaps, while code transformation techniques such as function permutation have not been realized.

Chongkyung et al. [24] address this shortcoming, and introduce address space layout permutation (ASLP), a fine-grained randomization scheme performing function permutation. The proposed scheme statically rewrites ELF executables to permute all functions and data objects of an application. Moreover, the underlying Linux kernel has been instrumented to increase the randomization entropy for the base address randomization of shared libraries.

Whereas Chongkyung et al. [24] target Linux and require accurate disassembly, Pappas et al. [27] explore fine-grained code randomization for Windows executables where no side information (e.g., relocation information) is available. Their tool, called ORP, randomizes instructions and registers within a basic block to mitigate return-oriented programming attacks, but leaves all functions at their original position. A more fine-grained randomization approach is taken by Hiser et al. [18]: instruction location randomization (ILR) randomizes the location of each single instruction in the virtual address space, while the execution is guided by a so-called fall-through map. For this, a program needs to be analyzed and re-assembled during a static analysis phase. In particular, the static analysis phase creates the fall-through map and applies binary rewriting to diversify the location of each instruction. However, ILR induces a high performance and file size overhead.

In general, static rewriting has one major limitation: a program will be only re-diversified if the static analysis phase is repeated. Static analysis may require a relatively long time to execute. For instance, in [18] it takes 36 s for only randomizing the binary. Hence, it is very likely that most program binaries will repeatedly execute with the same diversification layout, increasing the chance for an adversary to learn the program layout.

To tackle the limitation of only randomizing an application once, Wartell et al. [34] presented binary stirring (STIR) and Davi et al. [9] a load-time rewriter called XIFER. STIR and XIFER both perform basic block permutation for each application run. For this, STIR leverages static analysis and load-time randomization. In contrast, XIFER only applies load-time instrumentation. In the static analysis phase, STIR transforms the binary to facilitate load-time randomization. In particular, it creates a copy of the code section. The original code section is treated as a data-only section to preserve static data interleaved with code at its original address. In contrast, the copy of the code section is disassembled to allow load-time basic block randomization. At runtime, a trusted library takes control first and performs basic block permutation before the program starts executing. XIFER also keeps compatibility to static code signatures since it rewrites the binary in memory at load-time.

Whereas XIFER and STIR focus on randomizing basic blocks, Gupta et al. [17] focus on function permutation for Linux ELF binaries. Their fine-grained randomization scheme, called Marlin, identifies function blocks by using the public tool Unstrip, a tool that restores symbol information. Marlin is based on randomizing the functions' symbols to enable function permutation.

4.2 Just-in-Time Code-Reuse Attacks

Fine-grained code randomization schemes have been introduced to tackle the limitations of base address randomization. Indeed, with fine-grained code randomization enabled, an adversary cannot reliably determine the addresses of interesting gadgets based on disclosing a single runtime address. This is mainly due to the fact that existing code-reuse attacks require the adversary to perform static and offline analysis on the application's binary files to identify useful gadgets. Since ideal fine-grained code randomization performs code randomization at application load-time (e.g., as performed by XIFER [9] and STIR [34]), an adversary can hardly mount any code-reuse attack due to the lack of runtime information.

In order to perform a code-reuse attack on randomized code, an adversary needs to defer gadget discovery to application runtime. This is challenging since an adversary needs to locate and read valid code pages in memory. In addition, it requires a disassembly engine and a gadget finding tool which both need to be executed at runtime. On the other hand, many of the modern applications today feature a scripting engine to support client-side scripting, e.g., JavaScript for web browsers, VBScript for Microsoft Office applications, or ActionScript for Adobe Flash Player. That is, an adversary can execute some well-defined code (embedded into a script) on the target platform. Although scripting languages do not provide low-level interfaces to directly access and modify memory pages, they allow the attacker to instantiate a new class of code-reuse called just-in-time return-oriented programming (JIT-ROP) [31].

4.2.1 Assumptions and Adversary Model

In general, an adversary's actions may be enumerated in two stages: (1) exercise a vulnerable entry point, and (2) execute arbitrary malicious computations. Similar to previous work on runtime exploits, JIT-ROP assumes defense mechanisms for

the second stage of runtime exploits, *the execution of malicious computations.*
In particular, the target platform uses the following mechanisms to mitigate the
execution of malicious computations:

- **Data execution prevention:** The security model of data execution prevention
  is applied to the stack and the heap (cf. Sect. 2.4). Hence, the attacker is not
  able to inject code into the program's data area. Further, the same mechanism
  is applied to all executables and native system libraries, thereby preventing one
  from overwriting existing code.
- **Base address randomization:** The target platform deploys base address randomization by means of ASLR, and all useful, predictable, mappings have been
  eliminated.
- **Fine-grained ASLR:** The target platform enforces fine-grained code randomization on executables and libraries. In particular, a strong fine-grained randomization scheme is deployed, which (1) permutes the order of functions [5, 24]
  and basic blocks [9, 34], (2) swaps registers and replaces instructions [27], and
  (3) performs randomization upon each run of an application [9, 34].

Nevertheless, even given all these fortified defenses, the JIT-ROP attack framework can undermine the security provided by these techniques. JIT-ROP only
assumes that the adversary can disclose a single leaked runtime address (e.g., a
function pointer).

4.2.2 Basic Attack Principle

JIT-ROP circumvents fine-grained ASLR by finding gadgets and generating the
return-oriented payload on-the-fly at runtime. As for any other real-world code-
reuse attack, it only requires a memory disclosure of a *single* runtime address.
However, in contrast to standard code-reuse attacks against ASLR, JIT-ROP only
requires the runtime address of a valid code pointer, without knowing to which
precise code part or function it points to. Hence, JIT-ROP can use any code pointer
such as return addresses on the stack to instantiate the attack. Based on that leaked
address, JIT-ROP discloses the content of multiple memory pages and generates the
return-oriented payload at runtime. The detailed workflow of a JIT-ROP attack is
shown in Fig. 4.3.

First, the adversary exploits a memory disclosure vulnerability to retrieve the
runtime address of a code pointer (Step ❶). One of the main observations of JIT-
ROP is that the disclosed address will reside on a 4 KB-aligned memory page ($Page_0$
in Fig. 4.3). Hence, at runtime, the attacker can identify the start and end of $Page_0$
(Step ❷). Afterwards, JIT-ROP deploys a runtime disassembler, whose task is to
disassemble $Page_0$ on-the-fly (Step ❸). The disassembled page (Step ❹) provides
4 KB of gadget space, but more importantly, it will likely contain direct branch
instructions to other pages, e.g., a call to Func_B (Step ❺). Since Func_B resides
on another memory page (namely $Page_1$), JIT-ROP can again determine the page

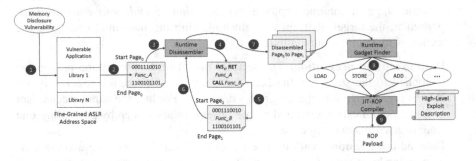

Fig. 4.3 Workflow of a JIT-ROP attack

start and end, and disassemble Page$_1$ (Step ❻). This procedure can be repeated as long as JIT-ROP identifies new direct branches pointing to yet undiscovered memory pages (Step ❼). Based on the disassembled pages, JIT-ROP deploys a runtime gadget finder to identify useful gadgets such as LOAD, STORE, or an ADD (Step ❽). Finally, JIT-ROP generates the return-oriented payload based on the discovered gadgets and a high-level description provided by the adversary (Step ❾). All the different components involved in a JIT-ROP attack are embedded into a single exploit file (such as a JavaScript file for browser-based attacks).

4.2.3   Implications

Due to the fact that JIT-ROP entirely performs at runtime and does not rely on any offline static analysis, it can circumvent conventional as well as fine-grained ASLR solutions. Since it also requires only a single code pointer to instantiate the attack (without precisely knowing to which specific code or function the code pointer points to), it seems very probable that JIT-ROP will soon be leveraged in real-world return-oriented exploits.

Snow et al. [31] show in their evaluation the power of JIT-ROP by exploiting Internet Explorer (IE) 8 running on Windows 7 based on CVE-2012-1876. As a proof-of-concept, the vulnerability is exploited to automatically load the Windows Calculator application upon browsing a HTML page. A memory disclosure vulnerability is exploited to instantiate the JIT-ROP attack allowing the attacker to harvest 301 code pages from the Internet Explorer process (including those pages harvested from library modules). That is, the attacker can disclose the content of ≈1.2 MB randomized code. The leaked code pages provided the attacker with a large code base (including a large amount of gadgets) to perform code-reuse attacks. In particular, JIT-ROP discovered many useful call sites to dangerous functions such as *LoadLibrary()* and *GetProcAddress()* which allow the attacker to invoke any function she desires. The number of code pages leaked naturally depends on the starting pointer. For the interested reader, Snow et al. [31] provide an extensive evaluation on how many pages and gadgets can be discovered starting code page harvesting from different pointers.

A knee-jerk reaction to mitigate JIT-ROP attacks is to simply re-randomize code pages at a high rate; doing so would render the attack ineffective as the disclosed pages might be re-randomized before the just-in-time payload executes. While this may indeed be one way forward, we expect that the re-randomization costs would make such a solution impractical. In fact, re-randomization is yet to be shown as an effective mechanism for user applications.

Another potential mitigation technique is instruction set randomization (ISR) (e.g., [3, 23]), which mitigates code injection attacks by encrypting the binary's code pages with a random key and decrypting them on-the-fly. Although ISR is a defense against code injection, it complicates code-reuse attacks when it is combined with fine-grained ASLR. In particular, it can complicate the gadget discovery process because the entire memory content is encrypted. On the other hand, ISR has been shown to be vulnerable to key guessing attacks [33, 35]—that become more powerful in the face of memory disclosure attacks like JIT-ROP, suffers from high performance penalties [3], or requires hardware assistance that is not yet present in commodity systems [23].

4.3   Advanced Code Randomization Schemes

Unfortunately, conventional approaches to fine-grained code randomization can be circumvented with JIT-ROP attacks. This is mainly due to the fact that randomization in these schemes only occurs once at compile-time or load-time. Hence, disclosure of a large amount of code pages allows an adversary to read randomized code and build a return-oriented exploit thereof.

To tackle the limitations of conventional code randomization schemes one could continuously re-randomize the program layout. That is, an adversary would still be able to read randomized code, but the randomized code is replaced before the adversary launches the return-oriented exploit. In fact, one of the schemes we have discussed above enables re-randomization: Giuffrida et al. [16] allow program modules of a microkernel to be re-randomized after a specified time period. Unfortunately, re-randomization induces significant runtime overhead, e.g., nearly 50 % overhead when applied every second.

As a matter of fact, the aforementioned ILR proposal suggested by Hiser et al. [18] cannot be directly bypassed by JIT-ROP attacks. This is because execution is guided based on a fall-through map that defines the successor instruction of each single instruction. On the other hand, as we discussed above, ILR suffers from several practical problems. As a consequence, a number of new and advanced code randomization schemes have been suggested to efficiently and effectively prevent JIT-ROP attacks.

Backes and Nürnberger [1] propose Oxymoron, a fine-grained code randomization scheme that enables code sharing for randomized shared libraries. In particular,

Oxymoron hides direct code references embedded in direct call and jump instructions to defend against JIT-ROP attacks. Recall that JIT-ROP attacks follow these references to identify and disassemble valid code pages. As such, the adversary is restricted to a single code page, i.e., the page that is referenced by the initial leaked pointer ($Page_0$ in Fig. 4.3). The hiding of these crucial references is achieved by means of memory segmentation on x86, and adding an extra layer of indirection. That is, direct calls and jumps are replaced with indirect calls and jumps that leverage a segment register and an index as their base register to redirect control-flow to a secret table that contains the original target addresses. Unfortunately, Oxymoron can be bypassed with an improved version of JIT-ROP attacks [10]: an attacker can harvest multiple function pointers and return addresses residing on the application's stack and heap. These pointers allow the attacker to reliably locate and disclose many code pages, and launch a return-oriented exploit.

The improved JIT-ROP attack is possible because code pages still remain readable in Oxymoron. Hence, any valid code pointer leads to a 4 KB code page that can be leveraged for a code-reuse attack. As a consequence, Backes et al. [2] set code pages to non-readable in a follow-up work. Their approach, denoted as eXecute-no-Read (XnR), sets all code pages except the page on which execution currently takes place to non-present. Hence, an adversary can only read from the currently executing code page, but not from any other page. A dedicated page fault handler is triggered whenever the program leaves the current page, and aims to execute code from a non-present page. In such cases, the non-present page is set to executable and readable, while the previous page is set to non-present. To improve performance, XnR keeps a window of multiple memory pages that are set to executable and readable. XnR is only effective against conventional code-reuse attacks if it is deployed in conjunction with a fine-grained randomization scheme. However, it remains unclear which randomization scheme is best suited to work in conjunction with XnR. Further, code pages, where execution currently takes place, still need to be mapped as readable. This allows an attacker to read the currently executing page. Gionta et al. [15] tackle this shortcoming by leveraging a split translation lookaside buffer (TLB) architecture which allows code pages to be only executable and not readable. However, split-TLB based architectures do no longer exist in modern processor architectures.

Recently, Crane et al. [8] investigated a hardware-based approach to enable execute-only memory. The introduced framework called Readactor leverages extended page tables (EPT) to conveniently mark memory pages as non-executable. In addition, the authors developed a LLVM-based compiler that (1) performs function permutation, (2) strictly separates code from data, and (3) hides code pointers. The latter is required to tackle entropy problems of several fine-grained randomization schemes. Consider a fine-grained randomization scheme that only performs randomization at the granularity of pages [1] or at the granularity of functions [24]. Although these schemes are more efficient than instruction-level randomization, they allow an attacker to determine a reasonable code base: given a single leaked function pointer, the attacker can statically determine all gadgets on the corresponding memory page (for page-level randomization), and all gadgets inside the corresponding function (for function-level randomization). In Readactor, these attacks are limited by introducing a layer of indirection. Specifically, it dispatches all indirect branches through dedicated non-readable trampolines. The attacker has only access to the trampoline addresses, but not to the actual runtime addresses of functions and call sites. However, the valid trampoline addresses provide a small code base which may be exploited for a code-reuse attack.

An alternative defense strategy has been proposed by Davi et al. [10]. Instead of marking memory as not-readable, they propose a hybrid approach which leverages code and execution path randomization. In particular, the framework, called Isomeron, dynamically randomizes the execution path between the original application and a diversified, but semantically equivalent application. At the granularity of function calls, Isomeron randomly decides whether to continue execution on the diversified or the original program image. This random decision is repeated whenever a function call occurs, and the execution diversifier ensures that a function is completely executed either from the original or diversified program image. This tolerates any memory disclosure of the program's executable code. However, due to dynamic binary instrumentation, Isomeron incurs performance overhead.

4.4 Conclusion and Summary

The principle of software diversity has recently facilitated the design and implementation of many new defenses against code-reuse attacks. In particular, fine-grained code randomization aims at significantly complicating code-reuse attacks which rely on statically determined code sequences (gadgets). We examined the underlying assumptions of fine-grained code randomization schemes, and noticed that they only defend against code-reuse attacks where the attacker determines gadgets within an offline static analysis phase. As a consequence, they can be circumvented by means of dynamic code-reuse attacks which determine gadgets on-the-fly without any static analysis. In particular, JIT-ROP attacks can be generated and applied to modern applications such as web browsers. JIT-ROP demonstrates that memory paging in modern processor architectures can be exploited to disclose the randomized code of many memory pages based on a single leaked runtime address. To tackle these novel code-reuse attacks, several improved code randomization schemes have been recently proposed. In principle, these schemes either mark memory as non-readable (i.e., execute-only) or combine code randomization with execution path randomization.

References

1. Backes, M., Nürnberger, S.: Oxymoron: making fine-grained memory randomization practical by allowing code sharing. In: Proceedings of the 23rd USENIX Security Symposium (2014). http://dl.acm.org/citation.cfm?id=2671225.2671253
2. Backes, M., Holz, T., Kollenda, B., Koppe, P., Nürnberger, S., Pewny, J.: You can run but you can't read: Preventing disclosure exploits in executable code. In: Proceedings of the 21st ACM Conference on Computer and Communications Security, CCS'14 (2014). http://doi.acm.org/10.1145/2660267.2660378

3. Barrantes, E.G., Ackley, D.H., Palmer, T.S., Stefanovic, D., Zovi, D.D.: Randomized instruction set emulation to disrupt binary code injection attacks. In: Proceedings of the 10th ACM Conference on Computer and Communications Security, CCS'03 (2003). http://doi.acm.org/10.1145/948109.948147

4. Bhatkar, S., DuVarney, D., Sekar, R.: Address obfuscation: an efficient approach to combat a broad range of memory error exploits. In: Proceedings of the 12th USENIX Security Symposium (2003). http://dl.acm.org/citation.cfm?id=1251353.1251361

5. Bhatkar, S., Sekar, R., DuVarney, D.C.: Efficient techniques for comprehensive protection from memory error exploits. In: Proceedings of the 14th USENIX Security Symposium (2005). http://dl.acm.org/citation.cfm?id=1251398.1251415

6. Bittau, A., Belay, A., Mashtizadeh, A., Mazières, D., Boneh, D.: Hacking blind. In: Proceedings of the 35th IEEE Symposium on Security and Privacy, SP'14 (2014). http://dx.doi.org/10.1109/SP.2014.22

7. Cohen, F.B.: Operating system protection through program evolution. Comput. Secur. **12**(6), 565–584 (1993). doi:10.1016/0167-4048(93)90054-9

8. Crane, S., Liebchen, C., Homescu, A., Davi, L., Larsen, P., Sadeghi, A.R., Brunthaler, S., Franz, M.: Readactor: practical code randomization resilient to memory disclosure. In: Proceedings of the 36th IEEE Symposium on Security and Privacy, SP'15 (2015) doi:10.1109/SP.2015.52

9. Davi, L., Dmitrienko, A., Nürnberger, S., Sadeghi, A.R.: Gadge me if you can - secure and efficient ad-hoc instruction-level randomization for x86 and ARM. In: Proceedings of the 8th ACM Symposium on Information, Computer and Communications Security, ASIACCS'13 (2013). http://doi.acm.org/10.1145/2484313.2484351

10. Davi, L., Liebchen, C., Sadeghi, A.R., Snow, K.Z., Monrose, F.: Isomeron: Code randomization resilient to (just-in-time) return-oriented programming. In: Proceedings of the 22nd Annual Network and Distributed System Security Symposium, NDSS'15 (2015). http://www.internetsociety.org/doc/isomeron-code-randomization-resilient-just-time-return-oriented-programming

11. Forrest, S., Somayaji, A., Ackley, D.: Building diverse computer systems. In: Proceedings of the 6th Workshop on Hot Topics in Operating Systems (HotOS-VI), HOTOS'97 (1997). http://dl.acm.org/citation.cfm?id=822075.822408

12. Franz, M.: E unibus pluram: massive-scale software diversity as a defense mechanism. In: Proceedings of the 2010 Workshop on New Security Paradigms, NSPW'10 (2010). http://doi.acm.org/10.1145/1900546.1900550

13. Fresi Roglia, G., Martignoni, L., Paleari, R., Bruschi, D.: Surgically returning to randomized lib(c). In: Proceedings of the 25th Annual Computer Security Applications Conference, ACSAC'09 (2009). http://dx.doi.org/10.1109/ACSAC.2009.16

14. gera: Advances in format string exploitation. Phrack Mag. **59**(12) (2002). http://www.phrack.com/issues.html?issue=59&id=7

15. Gionta, J., Enck, W., Ning, P.: HideM: protecting the contents of userspace memory in the face of disclosure vulnerabilities. In: Proceedings of the 5th ACM Conference on Data and Application Security and Privacy, CODASPY'15 (2015). http://doi.acm.org/10.1145/2699026.2699107

16. Giuffrida, C., Kuijsten, A., Tanenbaum, A.S.: Enhanced operating system security through efficient and fine-grained address space randomization. In: Proceedings of the 21st USENIX Security Symposium (2012). http://dl.acm.org/citation.cfm?id=2362793.2362833

17. Gupta, A., Kerr, S., Kirkpatrick, M., Bertino, E.: Marlin: a fine grained randomization approach to defend against ROP attacks. In: Network and System Security. Lecture Notes in Computer Science, vol. 7873 (2013). http://dx.doi.org/10.1007/978-3-642-38631-2_22

18. Hiser, J.D., Nguyen-Tuong, A., Co, M., Hall, M., Davidson, J.W.: ILR: Where'd my gadgets go? In: Proceedings of the 33rd IEEE Symposium on Security and Privacy, SP'12 (2012). http://dx.doi.org/10.1109/SP.2012.39

19. Homescu, A., Brunthaler, S., Larsen, P., Franz, M.: Librando: transparent code randomization for just-in-time compilers. In: Proceedings of the 20th ACM Conference on Computer and Communications Security, CCS'13 (2013). http://doi.acm.org/10.1145/2508859.2516675

20. Homescu, A., Neisius, S., Larsen, P., Brunthaler, S., Franz, M.: Profile-guided automated software diversity. In: Proceedings of the 2013 IEEE/ACM International Symposium on Code Generation and Optimization, CGO'13 (2013). http://dx.doi.org/10.1109/CGO.2013.6494997

21. Jackson, T., Salamat, B., Homescu, A., Manivannan, K., Wagner, G., Gal, A., Brunthaler, S., Wimmer, C., Franz, M.: Compiler-generated software diversity. In: Moving Target Defense. Advances in Information Security, vol. 54. Springer, New York (2011). http://dx.doi.org/10.1007/978-1-4614-0977-9_4

22. Jackson, T., Homescu, A., Crane, S., Larsen, P., Brunthaler, S., Franz, M.: Diversifying the software stack using randomized NOP insertion. In: Moving Target Defense II. Advances in Information Security, vol. 100. Springer, New York (2013). http://dx.doi.org/10.1007/978-1-4614-5416-8_8

23. Kc, G.S., Keromytis, A.D., Prevelakis, V.: Countering code-injection attacks with instruction-set randomization. In: Proceedings of the 10th ACM Conference on Computer and Communications Security, CCS'03 (2003). http://doi.acm.org/10.1145/948109.948146

24. Kil, C., Jun, J., Bookholt, C., Xu, J., Ning, P.: Address space layout permutation (ASLP): towards fine-grained randomization of commodity software. In: Proceedings of the 22nd Annual Computer Security Applications Conference, ACSAC'06 (2006). http://dx.doi.org/10.1109/ACSAC.2006.9

25. Larsen, P., Homescu, A., Brunthaler, S., Franz, M.: SoK: automated software diversity. In: Proceedings of the 35th IEEE Symposium on Security and Privacy, SP'14 (2014). http://dx.doi.org/10.1109/SP.2014.25

26. Liu, L., Han, J., Gao, D., Jing, J., Zha, D.: Launching return-oriented programming attacks against randomized relocatable executables. In: Proceedings of the 10th International Conference on Trust, Security and Privacy in Computing and Communications, TRUSTCOM'11 (2011). http://dx.doi.org/10.1109/TrustCom.2011.9

27. Pappas, V., Polychronakis, M., Keromytis, A.D.: Smashing the gadgets: hindering return-oriented programming using in-place code randomization. In: Proceedings of the 33rd IEEE Symposium on Security and Privacy, SP'12 (2012). http://dx.doi.org/10.1109/SP.2012.41

28. PaX Team: PaX address space layout randomization (ASLR). http://pax.grsecurity.net/docs/aslr.txt

29. Serna, F.J.: CVE-2012-0769, the case of the perfect info leak. http://zhodiac.hispahack.com/my-stuff/security/Flash_ASLR_bypass.pdf (2012)

30. Shacham, H., Jin Goh, E., Modadugu, N., Pfaff, B., Boneh, D.: On the effectiveness of address-space randomization. In: Proceedings of the 11th ACM Conference on Computer and Communications Security, CCS'04 (2004). http://doi.acm.org/10.1145/1030083.1030124

31. Snow, K.Z., Monrose, F., Davi, L., Dmitrienko, A., Liebchen, C., Sadeghi, A.R.: Just-in-time code reuse: on the effectiveness of fine-grained address space layout randomization. In: Proceedings of the 34th IEEE Symposium on Security and Privacy, SP'13 (2013). http://dx.doi.org/10.1109/SP.2013.45. Received the Best Student Paper Award

32. Sotirov, A., Dowd, M.: Bypassing browser memory protections in Windows Vista. http://www.phreedom.org/research/bypassing-browser-memory-protections/ (2008). Presented at Black Hat 2008

33. Sovarel, A.N., Evans, D., Paul, N.: Where's the FEEB? The effectiveness of instruction set randomization. In: Proceedings of the 14th USENIX Security Symposium (2005). http://dl.acm.org/citation.cfm?id=1251398.1251408

34. Wartell, R., Mohan, V., Hamlen, K.W., Lin, Z.: Binary stirring: self-randomizing instruction addresses of legacy x86 binary code. In: Proceedings of the 19th ACM Conference on Computer and Communications Security, CCS'12 (2012). http://doi.acm.org/10.1145/2382196.2382216

35. Weiss, Y., Barrantes, E.G.: Known/chosen key attacks against software instruction set randomization. In: Proceedings of the 22nd Annual Computer Security Applications Conference, ACSAC'06 (2006). http://dx.doi.org/10.1109/ACSAC.2006.33

Chapter 5
Discussion and Conclusion

Modern runtime exploits perform malicious program actions based on the principle of code-reuse. These attacks require no code injection, bypass widely deployed defense mechanisms, allow Turing-complete computation, can be applied to many processor architectures, and are highly challenging to prevent. Large-scale cyber attacks that have been recently discovered such as the well-known Stuxnet virus include code-reuse attack techniques [8].

As we have shown in this book, a large number of defenses and improved code-reuse attacks have appeared in the academic literature. Moreover, Microsoft recently released a new exploitation defense tool, called EMET, which includes a number of mitigation techniques to prevent runtime exploits [9]. Furthermore, the upcoming version of Windows 10 will include a new feature, called control-flow guard, which aims at enforcing control-flow checks for indirect calls to limit code-reuse attacks [10]. Google recently explored defenses against code-reuse attacks and introduced an instrumented compiler toolchain that enables control-flow checks for indirect calls [17].

5.1 Comparing Control-Flow Integrity and Code Randomization

In this book, we explored the most prominent defense principles against code-reuse attacks: control-flow integrity (CFI) [2] and software diversity [3] such as fine-grained code randomization. CFI is based on explicit checks, while software diversity relies on a secret, *i.e.*, the randomization offset for base address randomization, making code-reuse attacks highly cumbersome. Both approaches have their advantages and disadvantages. In the remainder of this section, we discuss and compare both defense approaches. We focus our discussion on security aspects since performance highly varies among different instantiations and deployed instrumentation techniques.

© The Author(s) 2015

L. Davi, A.-R. Sadeghi, *Building Secure Defenses Against Code-Reuse Attacks*,
SpringerBriefs in Computer Science, DOI 10.1007/978-3-319-25546-0_5

CFI provides provable security [1]. That is, one can formally verify that CFI enforcement is sound. In particular, the explicit control-flow checks inserted by CFI into an application provide strong assurance that a program's control-flow cannot be arbitrarily hijacked by an adversary. In contrast, code randomization does not put any restriction on the program's control-flow. In fact, the attacker can provide any valid memory address as an indirect branch target.

Both schemes assume that code is not writable. Hence, an attacker cannot simply replace the original code with malicious code. In addition, classic fine-grained code randomization schemes (cf. Sect. 4.1) assume that the adversary does not possess full knowledge of the program's memory layout. Otherwise, an attacker could leverage this information to perform just-in-time code-reuse attacks [15]. Due to explicit control-flow checks full knowledge of the program's memory layout still does not allow an attacker to undermine CFI protection. Another related problem of protection schemes based on code randomization are side-channel attacks [6, 14]. These attacks exploit timing and fault analysis side channels to infer randomization information.

On the other hand, CFI relies on the precision of the application's control-flow graph (CFG). If valid branch addresses cannot be identified during static analysis, CFI needs to make security compromises, and expands the set of valid addresses to preserve the program's functionality. In the worst-case, this taken compromise introduces malicious control-flow paths that an attacker can exploit. In particular, coarse-grained CFI solutions that intentionally allow many branch addresses introduce a large number of new control-flow paths that an attacker can exploit. For instance, many CFI schemes allow return instructions to target any call-preceded instruction [12, 19]. Such coarse-grained policies allow an attacker to construct return-oriented exploits from legitimate control-flow paths as we have shown in Sect. 3.2.

CFG imprecision allows an attacker to easily generate generic attack vectors that can be mounted on all computer systems that deploy the CFI-protected software program. This is not directly possible if programs are protected with fine-grained code randomization, because the code layout will differ for each platform.

In conclusion, CFI provides stronger security guarantees than code randomization schemes. However, CFI relies on an accurate and precise CFG. If the CFG is incomplete or includes too many valid control-flow paths, fine-grained code randomization can provide better security.

Recently, several defense mechanisms started to combine CFI with code randomization. For instance, Zhang et al. [20] allocate for each possible branch target a code stub on a Springboard section. All code stubs on the Springboard section are randomized to prevent an adversary from exploiting code stubs to construct return-oriented exploits. In particular, Mohan et al. [11] present the design and implementation of opaque CFI (O-CFI). This binary instrumentation-based solution leverages coarse-grained CFI checks and code randomization to prevent return-oriented exploits. For this, O-CFI identifies a unique set of possible target addresses for each indirect branch instruction. Afterwards, it uses the per-indirect branch set to restrict the target address of the indirect branch to only its minimal and maximal members. To further reduce the set of possible addresses, it arranges basic blocks belonging to an indirect branch set into clusters (so that they are located nearby to each other), and also randomizes their location. However, O-CFI relies on precise static analysis. In particular, it statically determines valid branch addresses for return instructions. Nevertheless, Mohan et al. [11] demonstrate that combining CFI with code randomization is a promising research direction.

5.2 Future Research Directions

Preventing Return-Into-libc Attacks Most proposed CFI and fine-grained code randomization defenses focus on the detection and prevention of return-oriented programming attacks, but do not provide full protection against return-into-libc attacks. This is only natural, given the fact that the majority of code-reuse attacks require a few return-oriented gadgets to initialize registers and prepare memory before calling a system call or critical function. However, Schuster et al. [13] have recently demonstrated that code-reuse attacks based on only calling a chain of virtual methods allow arbitrary malicious program actions. In addition, Tran et al. [18] have demonstrated that pure return-into-libc attacks can achieve Turing-completeness. Detecting such attacks is highly challenging: modern programs link to a large number of libraries, and require dangerous API and system calls to operate correctly [5]. Hence, for these programs, dangerous API and system calls are legitimate control-flow targets for indirect and direct call instructions; even if fine-grained CFI policies are enforced. In order to detect code-reuse attacks that exploit these functions, CFI needs to be combined with additional security checks, *e.g.*, with dynamic taint analysis or techniques to perform argument validation. We believe that developing such CFI extensions is an important future research direction.

Memory Safety In this book, we have focused on the second stage of runtime exploits, *i.e.*, the malicious computation after the control-flow of a program has been hijacked. Until recently, defenses that aim at preventing the first stage of a runtime exploit, *i.e.*, the initial code pointer overwrite, were either incomplete or incurred too high performance overhead. Recently, Szekeres et al. [16] presented the idea of code pointer integrity (CPI), and its implementation on x86 and x86-64 [7]. CPI separates code pointers as well as pointers to code pointers in a safe memory region that can only be accessed by instructions that are proven to be safe at compile-time. CPI operates very efficient on C code, but may incur performance overhead of more than 40 % for C++-compiled code. With respect to security, CPI relies on the protection of the safe memory region which is efficiently possible on x86 leveraging segmentation. However, on x86-64 where segmentation is not fully available, CPI relies on hiding the safe memory region. Unfortunately, Evans et al. [4] have recently demonstrated that side-channel attacks can be leveraged against one of the x86-64 CPI implementations to locate and alter the safe memory region. Given the new approaches and attacks in this area, we believe that defenses that aim at memory safety for type-unsafe languages are a promising future research direction.

Hardware Support Mitigation of runtime exploits by means of software-only based approaches often incurs unacceptable high performance overhead. To address this practical shortcoming, hardware manufactures have recently released a number of hardware features enabling efficient prevention of runtime exploits. For instance, data execution prevention is today enabled on almost every system because all of the major hardware manufactures feature the non-executable bit. Other examples include the Memory Protection Extensions (MPX) on x86 to prevent buffer overflows, or SPARC's realtime Application Data Integrity (ADI) feature which aims at preventing buffer overflows and memory references bugs. Furthermore, processor manufactures are designing and developing CFI instructions to tackle the performance overhead of software-based CFI schemes. Hence, we believe that hardware/software co-design is a promising research detection to efficiently and effectively prevent code-reuse attacks.

5.3   Conclusion

Although memory corruption attacks are known for almost three decades, they are still a prevalent attack vector today. While conventional attacks required the injection of malicious code, state-of-the-art attacks reuse existing, benign code to launch malicious program actions. In this book, we explored the challenge of designing and building secure defenses against these so-called code-reuse attacks. In particular, we elaborated on two defense strategies: CFI and software diversity such as code randomization. As we have shown, both techniques are capable of effectively preventing code-reuse attacks, and significantly raise the bar for successful exploitation. However, due to legacy compliance and high performance requirements, many of the proposed defenses relax their security policies resulting in coarse-grained, and all too often, insecure protection. On the other hand, the good news is that building secure defenses against these attacks has become a very active research field at the time of writing this book. Further, well-known companies such as Google, Microsoft, Oracle, and Intel take the problem of memory corruption attacks seriously, and actively conduct research as well as build new innovative defenses.

References

1. Abadi, M., Budiu, M., Erlingsson, Ú., Ligatti, J.: A theory of secure control-flow.   In: Proceedings of the 7th International Conference on Formal Methods and Software Engineering, ICFEM'05 (2005). URL http://dx.doi.org/10.1007/11576280_9
2. Abadi, M., Budiu, M., Erlingsson, U., Ligatti, J.: Control-flow integrity: principles, implementations, and applications.   ACM Trans. Inf. Syst. Secur. **13**(1), 4:1–4:40 (2009).   URL http://doi.acm.org/10.1145/1609956.1609960

3. Cohen, F.B.: Operating system protection through program evolution. Comput. Secur. **12**(6), 565–584 (1993). doi:10.1016/0167-4048(93)90054-9

4. Evans, I., Fingeret, S., Gonzalez, J., Otgonbaatar, U., Tang, T., Shrobe, H., Sidiroglou-Douskos, S., Rinard, M., Okhravi, H.: Missing the point(er): on the effectiveness of code pointer integrity. In: Proceedings of the 36th IEEE Symposium on Security and Privacy, SP'15 (2015). doi:10.1109/SP.2015.51

5. Göktas, E., Athanasopoulos, E., Bos, H., Portokalidis, G.: Out of control: overcoming control-flow integrity. In: Proceedings of the 35th IEEE Symposium on Security and Privacy, SP'14 (2014). URL http://dx.doi.org/10.1109/SP.2014.43

6. Hund, R., Willems, C., Holz, T.: Practical timing side channel attacks against kernel space aslr. In: Proceedings of the 34th IEEE Symposium on Security and Privacy, SP'13 (2013). URL http://dx.doi.org/10.1109/SP.2013.23

7. Kuznetsov, V., Szekeres, L., Payer, M., Candea, G., Sekar, R., Song, D.: Code-pointer integrity. In: Proceedings of the 11th USENIX Conference on Operating Systems Design and Implementation, OSDI'14 (2014). URL http://dl.acm.org/citation.cfm?id=2685048.2685061

8. Matrosov, A., Rodionov, E., Harley, D., Malcho, J.: Stuxnet under the microscope (2001). URL http://www.esetnod32.ru/company/viruslab/analytics/doc/Stuxnet_Under_the_Microscope.pdf

9. Microsoft: Enhanced Mitigation Experience Toolkit. URL https://www.microsoft.com/emet

10. Microsoft Corporation: Visual Studio 2015 preview: work-in-progress security feature (2014). URL http://blogs.msdn.com/b/vcblog/archive/2014/12/08/visual-studio-2015-preview-work-in-progress-security-feature.aspx

11. Mohan, V., Larsen, P., Brunthaler, S., Hamlen, K.W., Franz, M.: Opaque control-flow integrity. In: Proceedings of the 22nd Annual Network and Distributed System Security Symposium, NDSS'15 (2015). URL http://www.internetsociety.org/doc/opaque-control-flow-integrity

12. Pappas, V., Polychronakis, M., Keromytis, A.D.: Transparent ROP exploit mitigation using indirect branch tracing. In: Proceedings of the 22nd USENIX Security Symposium (2013). URL http://dl.acm.org/citation.cfm?id=2534766.2534805

13. Schuster, F., Tendyck, T., Liebchen, C., Davi, L., Sadeghi, A.R., Holz, T.: Counterfeit object-oriented programming: On the difficulty of preventing code reuse attacks in C++ applications. In: Proceedings of the 36th IEEE Symposium on Security and Privacy, SP'15 (2015) doi:10.1109/SP.2015.51

14. Seibert, J., Okhravi, H., Söderström, E.: Information leaks without memory disclosures: Remote side channel attacks on diversified code. In: Proceedings of the 21st ACM SIGSAC Conference on Computer and Communications Security, CCS'14 (2014). URL http://doi.acm.org/10.1145/2660267.2660309

15. Snow, K.Z., Monrose, F., Davi, L., Dmitrienko, A., Liebchen, C., Sadeghi, A.R.: Just-in-time code reuse: on the effectiveness of fine-grained address space layout randomization. In: Proceedings of the 34th IEEE Symposium on Security and Privacy, SP'13 (2013). URL http://dx.doi.org/10.1109/SP.2013.45. Received the Best Student Paper Award

16. Szekeres, L., Payer, M., Wei, T., Song, D.: Sok: Eternal war in memory. In: Proceedings of the 34th IEEE Symposium on Security and Privacy, SP'13 (2013). URL http://dx.doi.org/10.1109/SP.2013.13

17. Tice, C., Roeder, T., Collingbourne, P., Checkoway, S., Erlingsson, Ú., Lozano, L., Pike, G.: Enforcing forward-edge control-flow integrity in GCC & LLVM. In: Proceedings of the 23rd USENIX Security Symposium (2014). URL http://dl.acm.org/citation.cfm?id=2671225.2671285

18. Tran, M., Etheridge, M., Bletsch, T., Jiang, X., Freeh, V., Ning, P.: On the expressiveness of return-into-libc attacks. In: Proceedings of the 14th International Conference on Recent Advances in Intrusion Detection, RAID'11 (2011). URL http://dx.doi.org/10.1007/978-3-642-23644-0_7

19. Zhang, M., Sekar, R.: Control flow integrity for COTS binaries. In: Proceedings of the 22nd USENIX Security Symposium (2013). URL http://dl.acm.org/citation.cfm?id=2534766. 2534796
20. Zhang, C., Wei, T., Chen, Z., Duan, L., Szekeres, L., McCamant, S., Song, D., Zou, W.: Practical control flow integrity & randomization for binary executables. In: Proceedings of the 34th IEEE Symposium on Security and Privacy, SP'13 (2013). URL http://dx.doi.org/10. 1109/SP.2013.44

Printed in the United States
By Bookmasters